bead embroidery stitch samples

YASUKO ENDO, CRK DESIGN

Bead Embroidery Stitch Samples
by CRK design /Yasuko Endo

First designed and published in Japan in 2011
by Graphic-sha Publishing Co., Ltd.
1-14-17 Kudan-kita, Chiyoda-ku,
Tokyo 102-0073 Japan

Text, images and design
© 2011 Yasuko Endo
© 2011 CRK design
© 2011 Graphic-sha Publishing Co., Ltd.

English language edition published in 2012
by Interweave Press LLC

First published in the United States of America by
Interweave Press LLC
201 East Fourth Street
Loveland, CO 80537-5655

ISBN-13: 978-1-59668-706-6

10 9 8 7 6 5 4 3 2 1

Library of Congress Cataloging-in-Publication Data
Yasuko Endo/ CRK design
Bead Embroidery Stitch Samples by CRK design/Yasuko Endo
pages cm
Summary: "Combine your love for hand stitching with beautiful beads to make delightfully original trims and embellishments' ̄- Provided by publisher.
Includes bibliographical references and index.
ISBN 978-1-5668-706-6 (pbk.)
1. Crafts-Jewelry 2. Beadwork - Patterns
Title. III Title: Bead Embroidery Stitch Samples.

Planning, production, editing & book design:	Chiaki Kitaya, Yasuko Endo and Kuma Imamura (CRK design)
Stitch design & piece production:	Yasuko Endo (CRK design)
Alphabet design:	Kaoru Emoto (CRK design)
Cooperation to piece production:	Midori Nishida, Setsuko Ishii, Takako Nogi and Yoko Ogawa
Photography:	Yoshiharu Ohtaki (studio seek)
Procedure photography:	Nobuei Araki (studio seek)
Styling:	CRK design
Model:	Masumi Minato
Editing and illustration for Lesson Note pages:	Kuma Imamura (CRK design)
Cooperation to editing & illustrations:	Tomoko Kajiyama
Cooperation to photo shooting:	AWABEES

English edition
Layout:	Shinichi Ishioka
Translation:	Sean Gaston, Yuko Wada, Takako Otomo
Editing and production:	Kumiko Sakamoto (Graphic-sha Publishing Co., Ltd.)

Printed and bound in China

CONTENTS

BASIC LESSON

6 Materials and Tools

8 Basics of Embroidery

13 Customize a T-shirt

14 Let's Start our Bead Embroidery Stitches

16 Running Stitches
stitch designs 1-6

LESSON-1

20 Straight Stitches
stitch designs 7-13

22 Back/Pekinese Stitches
stitch designs 14-20

24 Outline/Holbein Stitches
stitch designs 21-27

26 Blanket/Buttonhole Stitches
stitch designs 28-34

LESSON-2

30 Lazy Daisy Stitches
stitch designs 35-41

32 Chain Stitches
stitch designs 42-48

34 Cross Stitches
stitch designs 49-55

36 Chevron/Herringbone Stitches
stitch designs 56-62

38 Fern/Fly Stitches
stitch designs 63-69

40 Couching Stitches
stitch designs 70-76

42 Open Cretan Stitches
stitch designs 77-83

44 Zigzag Stitches
stitch designs 84-90

46 Feather Stitches
stitch designs 91-97

LESSON-3

50 Lace Motifs
stitch designs 98-111

54 Edging Stitches
stitch designs 112-118

56 Filling Stitches
stitch designs 119-124

58 One Point Motif
stitch designs 125-130

DESIGN CHARTS

60 Alphabet A to Z

62 Nordic Motifs

LESSON NOTES

65 How to Stitch with Beads

88 Recommended Combinations of Needles,
Threads, and Beads

Materials and Tools
Basics of Embroidery: How to Cross Stitch
Beginners Lesson: Customize a T-shirt
Running Stitches with Beads

BASIC LESSON

Linen shirt on the left page: Collar <stitch design 51> DMC #8/ECRU (natural undyed color), B5200 (white)/round bead 8/0 (3.0mm) No. 122 (milk), fly <stitch design 52> DMC #8/ECRU (natural undyed color)/round bead 8/0 (3.0mm) No. 122 (milk), sleeve edge <stitch design 56> DMC #8/ECRU (natural undyed color)/round bead 8/0 (3.0mm) No. 122 (milk), camisole: neckline <stitch design 52> DMC #8/ECRU (natural undyed color)/round bead No.122 (milk), front <stitch design in page 60> DMC #25/739 (beige, triple yarn)/round bead 8/0 (3.0mm) No.557 (gold)

Raffia hat: <stitch design 32> DMC #25/3864 (beige, double yarn)/round bead 11/0 (2.2mm) No.173 (yellow), 3mm-long bugle bead No. 7 (green), 6mm-long bugle bead No. 111 (thick yellow), <stitch design 78> DMC#25/3863 (light brown, quadruple yarn)/round bead 8/0 (3.0mm) No. 174 (orange), No. 105 (lime green)

Ribbon on the jam jar: Left <stitch designs 65 & 63> DMC#25/841 (beige)/round bead 11/0 (2.2mm) No. 105 (lime green), No. 174 (orange), No. 332 (purple-red), No. 402 (yellow), No. 405 (red), round bead No. 105 (lime green), Middle <stitch design 89> DMC #25/841 (beige)/round bead 11/0 (2.2mm) No. 105 (lime green), No. 332 (purple-red), No. 111 (thick yellow), No. 402 (yellow), No. 405 (red), Right <stitch design 64> DMC#25/3347 (green)/round bead 11/0 (2.2mm) No. 332 (purple-red), No. 405 (red)
*All yarn threads are quadrupled.

Materials and Tools

Shiny thick cotton thread with a wide color palette.

Embroidery thread #8

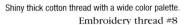

Embroidery thread #12

Shiny thin cotton thread.

Beads and Spangles

Round beads 8/0 (3.0mm)

Round beads 11/0 (2.2mm)

Bugle beads (3mm-long/6mm-long)

Magatama beads

Pearl beads

Spangles

Threads

DMC#25
Embroidery Thread

DMC #25 embroidery thread is good quality and its greatest appeal is the fine color variation of 465 colors. It is washfast and wears well, and keeps the good looks of the finished work. Use the six-ply thread and vary the number of yarn threads to fit the work.

Embroidery thread #25

Six-ply floss.

Embroidery thread #5

Bundled thick cotton thread.

Appleton Crewel wool embroidery thread

Wool embroidery thread with a fluffy texture. It includes a wide range of colors that go from pale to vivid colors.

Hemp yarn

Linen yarn with natural texture.

Sewing yarn #60

Double the yarn when sewing spangles.

TOHO Beads

These are best quality glass beads that come in assorted shapes. One feature is good-sized holes, which allow needles to pass smoothly. The beads also go well with threads of various materials. You can enjoy re-fashioning items with expressive beads and spangles and an assortment of stitches.

Fabrics

**DMC
needlework fabrics**

High-quality linen fabric for embroidery. 28- and 32-count fabrics are available.

**DMC
printed needlework fabrics**

14-count border print fabric. Pink and white and blue and white prints are available.

Needles

Clover Embroidery Needles

These are recommended for embroidery with beads. The needle tip is pointed and it goes through fabric smoothly. An "Assortment pack" is useful because you can use the best needle depending on the gauge and number of yarn threads used. Please refer to page 86 for the correspondence table with beads and embroidery threads.

Fusible interfacing for embroidery

This is useful when you stitch on stretchy fabric such as knits. Iron it onto the reverse side of the fabric to temporarily stabilize and make it easier to stitch.

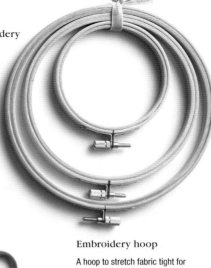

Embroidery needles with a round end

A "thin needle assortment pack" is good for small round beads, and a "thick needle assortment pack" is best for thick threads. The needle tip is round and causes less split yarn. The head part (with the hole) is thin and it passes through beads smoothly.

Bead embroidery needles

Needles for delicate bead embroidery. Useful for sewing spangles or small round beads with sewing yarn.

Cross-stitch needles

Needles with a blunt end for cross-stitch. It causes less split yarn in weaving yarns and embroidery threads when stitching.

Scissors

Small scissors with sharp points are recommended for cutting accurately.

Embroidery hoop

A hoop to stretch fabric tight for stitching. Move it around as you proceed with the chart.

Plotting scale

Bicolored scale which can be used according to the color of the fabric. It is flexible and useful for measuring curved parts or marking up fabric.

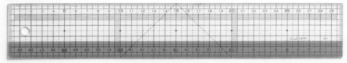

Tracer

Use it with paper chalk to copy detailed patterns. You can also use a ballpoint pen that has run out of ink.

Pencil-type chalk

Chalk in the shape of a pencil, useful for marking up dark colored fabric. It comes out easily with the accompanying brush.

Stamps

DMC's original alphabet stamps. You can use them to stamp ink on fabrics as a design and sew beads onto it, or to stamp as a pattern with disappearing ink.

Waste canvas

This is useful for doing a counted cross stitch on a fabric where the grain can't be counted. After stitching, mist it with water and remove it.

Paper chalk (one side type)

Use this to copy a pattern. Apply the transfer side to the fabric, place the pattern and cellophane on and trace around it with tracer or ballpoint pen which has run out of ink.

Water-soluble marker (with eraser)

You can mark up the fabric clearly with this useful marker, and it comes out with water. You can erase any part quickly with the accompanying eraser.

Threads   Tip – Wash your hands well before beggining to stitch.

Embroidery thread #25

Made by twisting together 6 slender threads. Pull the desired number of slender threads to control its thickness. For example, a "double yarn" refers to a thread made by bundling together two of these threads.

1 Pull out the thread #25 and cut it into 45-50 cm (17 3/4" - 19 5/8") length. If it is too long, the thread may fray or spoil easily.

2 Pull out the required number of slender threads one by one. Even if using it as a sextuple yarn, remove all one by one and re-bundle them.

3 Bundle together the required number of slender threads, aligning the ends.

Crewel wool embroidery thread

To make threading a needle with this thick wool embroidery thread easier, use a threader or a sewing yarn as the following figure shows.

4 Fold the bundled thread over a needle and pull the needle in the direction of the arrow, holding the thread firmly.

5 Insert the folded part of the thread into the needle hole.

6 Pull one end of the thread through and keep the length of the shorter thread about 10 cm (3 7/8").

Embroidery thread #5

A loop of a bundled single long thick thread. Cut thread to a length easy for use later.

1 Remove the labels and loosen the loop of twisted thread bundle.

2 Cut the knot part tying the thread together.

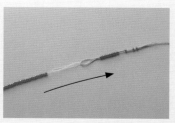

A label with the color number.

3 Thread the label with the bundle again and tie it loosely into a braid. Pull out thread from the folded part one by one for use in embroidery.

Beads   Tip – Choose packed loose beads or threaded beads according to your needs.

Loose beads

Separate and keep beads in a small container by type. Useful when you would like to use a small amount.

Threaded beads

Threading the embroidery thread

Useful for embroidery needing much bead-threading beforehand, such as couching stitches. Make an untiable loop at the bead-threaded string end and pass about 10 cm of thread through.

Move beads onto the embroidery thread. Maintain a slow pace to ensure the embroidery thread stays on and beads do not come off.

Marking and Tracing

Tip – Marking, tracing and other tools used differ depending on the pattern or embroidery fabric.

Marking with dots and lines

Lines and dots can be used as a guide showing the width or interval of stitches.

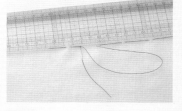

Water-soluble marker (with eraser)
For normal fabric such as cotton or linen. You can erase any part quickly using water or the accompanying eraser.

Pencil-type chalk
Useful for marking up dark color fabric. It comes out easily with your fingers or the accompanying brush.

Threads
For fabric on which markers, including pencil-type chalks, are unusable, mark by sewing with thread such as a sewing yarn.

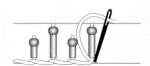

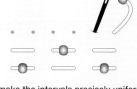

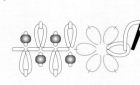

To align the width of stitches exactly, draw solid lines.

To make the intervals precisely uniform, mark with dots to guide points to insert a needle.

To make stitch shapes uniform, trace the pattern accurately.

Trace patterns

To trace the shape of stitches precisely, use a paper chalk (one sided type). Trace patterns, fixing the paper chalk firmly with pins or tape.

① Trace patterns on thin paper such as a tracing paper.

② Apply the transferable side to the fabric and lay the traced patterns on it. Place cellophane on this to smooth the surface and copy the patterns on with a tracer.

③ After tracing, check to ensure important patterns such as flower petals are traced fully, and you can determine points to insert a needle for regular and repeating motifs.

Embroidery Hoop

Tip – When working on small patterns or stable fabrics, it may be enough to stretch the fabric with your fingers without using this tool.

Setting up a tambour

This hoop is useful when using thin or loose fabric, or embroidery involving counting the number of grains, such as cross stitches.

① To protect and fix an embroidery fabric, wrap a bias-cut fabric around the inner hoop.

② Encase fabric on the inner hoop in the outer hoop, fixing by screwing. Cover the beaded part on hoop with another fabric, fixing loosely to the outer hoop.

③ Pull the fabric along the grain evenly to make it easier to insert the needle. Then be careful not to distort the grain.

*The pattern is shown on page 60.

Count the grain on the fabric to make an even cross shape. Always stitch the upper thread in the same direction to create a beautiful finish.

Pattern indication

Redbox, shows the X of the stitch and yellow circle, ◉ shows the part to place the beads. The size of the stitch changes depending on the number of weaving yarns chosen.

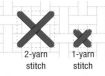

2-yarn stitch   1-yarn stitch

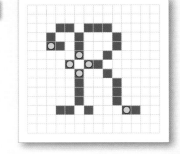

Stitch the letter R

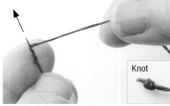

① Holding the thread end with the needle, wrap the thread around it a few times and pull the needle out.

Knot

② Bring the needle down to the back of the fabric and bring the needle up from the back at the starting point.

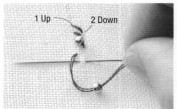

③ Stitch continuously in a vertical direction. When you want to place a bead, bring the needle up from the back to put it on..

④ Work back to complete the Xs. Please refer to Tips below for the bead part.

How to stitch

Stitch X continuously and vertically

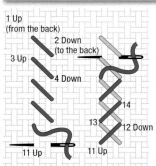

1 Up (from the back)
2 Down (to the back)
3 Up
4 Down
14
13
12 Down
11 Up   11 Up

Work a row of half stitches first, then work back to complete the X. This method is efficient when stitches are continuous or when you want to fill in the surface.

Complete each X

Stitch each X as you go.

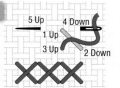

5 Up   4 Down
1 Up
3 Up   2 Down

Tips

Fix beads

Use this method to fix beads firmly without tilt.

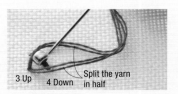

1 Up
2 Down

1 Take a bead and work a half stitch.

3 Up   4 Down   Split the yarn in half

2 Split the yarn in half with the bead at the center and complete the X.

3 Both sides of the bead are firmly fixed.

Stamp

Cross stitch stamp

Use a stamp instead of patterns and you can cross stitch a fabric on which it is difficult to count the grain.

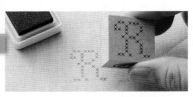

1 Stamp with fabric ink in a color similar to the thread or use disappearing ink.

2 Insert the needle in between the Xs.

You can also use the stamped mark as is and top it with beads.

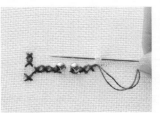

5 Turn the fabric to facilitate stitching.

6 Place the bead in the center and proceed from left to right.

7 Return to the left to complete the Xs.

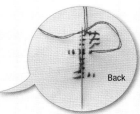

Back

When the remaining thread is 7cm (2 3/4") to 8cm (3 1/8"), make a knot on the back and hide the thread end in the stitches.

Back

To move to a part of the design using the same colored thread, but farther away, pass the thread through stitches on the back.

8 Stitch the right part of the letter.

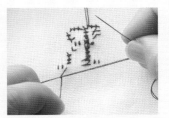

9 Make a knot on the back at the end. If using an open weave fabric, fasten it to a stitch on the back.

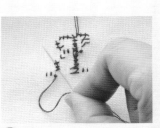

10 Hide the thread end in the stitches and cut the extra thread.

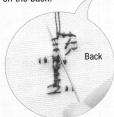

Back

When you start with new thread, loop it through the stitches on the back and then let out the thread on the top.

Completed!

Top

Back

Cut the knot you made at the start of stitching and draw the thread through the back. Fasten it to a stitch and hide the thread end in the stitches.

Basics of Embroidery   Additional techniques to make it more fun

Technique 1   Do a counted cross stitch on any fabric

You can stitch in the normal way on a fabric which has too tight a weave to count grain.

Waste canvas

Tack it temporarily to a fabric to make it easier to count the grain. After stitching, remove the waste canvas yarn. Since waste canvases of various sizes are available, select one based on pattern and thickness of thread.
*This is useful for cross stitch, Holbein stitch, herringbone stitch, zigzag stitch, etc.

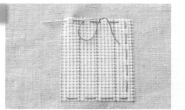
1 Cut waste canvas to a size slightly larger than the pattern, and tack it to the fabric.

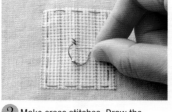
2 Make cross stitches. Draw the thread a little tight because the waste canvas will be removed later.

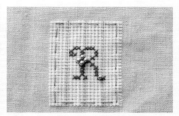
3 Stitch a letter.

4 Mist the whole area with water to melt away the starch of the waste canvas.

5 Remove the weaving yarn of the waste canvas one by one.

6 Complete.

Technique 2   Stitching on knits   Put fusible interfacing or Japanese paper on a soft and stretchy fabric.

Affix fusible interfacing

Using an iron at low heat, temporarily affix fusible interfacing to a stretchy fabric, so that the fabric doesn't stretch and becomes easily stitchable. You can also tack with Japanese paper.

1 Cut fusible interfacing to a size slightly larger than the pattern, and affix it to the fabric temporarily using an iron at low heat.

2 After stitching, tear and remove the fusible interfacing carefully. Take care not to pull the thread.

3 Complete. The thread is not too loose or tight.

Technique 3   When running out of thread   Continue with new thread to avoid any strange gaps in the pattern.

Join threads in the middle of stitching

When you do stitches that require wrapping the thread around needle, for example chain stitch, fly stitch or buttonhole stitch, join a new thread linking patterns.

1 Make the last stitch loose with no knot at the thread end on the back.

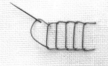
2 Insert the needle with a new thread, wrapping the last stitch around it.

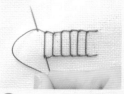
3 Make the next stitch, pulling the thread from the back to adjust, then finish the end.

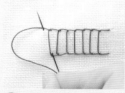
4 Continue stitching the pattern with the new thread.

BEGINNER'S LESSON
Customize a T-shirt

You can make 3-dimensional patterns just by threading beads onto the yarn.
Enjoy remaking your T-shirt by embellishing with easy needlework.

Striped shirt -- Collar <stitch design 2> DMC #5/552 (purple) / round bead 8/0
(3.0mm) No.23 (aqua), 402 (yellow) / Chest: <stitch design 6> DMC #5/517
(blue) / round bead 8/0 (3.0mm) No.264 (turquoise blue), 402 (yellow)
For the gray T-shirt, see page 14.

Let's start our bead embroidery stitches

Embellish your T-shirt design any way you want with beads and embroidery threads.
Enjoy color combining with different threads and beads.

A simple T-shirt for kids. It's all right to stitch around the neckline if the shoulder opens or the neckline is wide.

Material	
●	T-shirt
●	Embroidery thread: DMC #5/No. 517 (blue), No. 321 (red), No. 552 (purple)
●	Bead: TOHO round bead 8/0 (3.0mm) No. 23 (aqua), No. 405 (red), No. 402 (yellow), No. 264 (turquoise blue)
●	Needle: Clover embroidery needle with blunt tip (0.84mm)
●	Water-soluble marker (with eraser), scale, scissors

How to mark

15 mm (5/8")

5 mm (1/5") 15 mm (5/8")
15 mm (5/8")
10 mm (3/8") 25 mm (1")

Armpit

1 Mark (points) on neckline and chest at 1.5cm (5/8") intervals (see figure at left). For the chest, armpit is the base point.

Neckline

Neckline

Shoulder

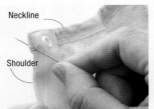

3 Insert the needle from the back so that the knot is hidden in the seam allowance or switching part.

2 Make a knot (see p.10) for thread passed through a needle. The size depends on how many times the thread is wrapped around the needle.

4 Draw the needle out from the best position to start stitching on the top.

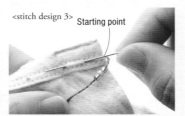

<stitch design 3> Starting point

5 Thread 3 beads, insert the needle in btwn two marks, then draw it out from the 2nd mark. Repeat this.

6 Stitch up to the opposite shoulder, then make a knot on the back after stitching once or twice on the seam allowance.

7 Stitching on the neckline is complete.

My motif
Make your own mark

Place a small cherry made up of beads instead of a name. This is a cute "mark" which will please the kids.

Material
● Embroidery thread: DMC #5/No. 164 (grass green)
● Bead: TOHO magatama bead 4mm (1/8")/M25 (red)
● Needle: Clover embroidery needle with blunt end (0.84mm)

Life-size pattern
● Leaves are drawn in lines for reference.
● Points show the position to insert the needle to make stems.

Utilize the pattern

Stripe or checked patterns can be used as a guide to stitch in a regular manner.

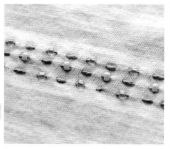

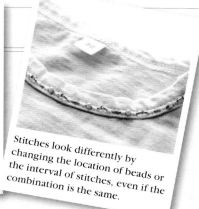

Stitch the upper and the lower edges of a the striped line and then stitch the middle of the line.

Stitches look differently by changing the location of beads or the interval of stitches, even if the combination is the same.

Chest

(8) Stitch once or twice along the armpit seam allowance and bring the needle up from the back at the start point.

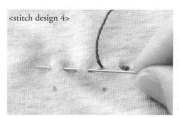

<stitch design 4>

(9) For the top pattern, make 2 aligned running stitch rows, then make a knot on the opposite armpit seam allowance.

(10) Make running stitches in between the two running stitch rows, inserting beads one by one and displacing the needle insertion points.

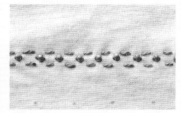

(11) The top pattern is complete.

<stitch design 5>

(12) To stitch the middle pattern, work 3 aligned rows of running stitch. Insert a bead every other stitch.

<>stitch design 1>

(13) For the bottom pattern, make running stitches, inserting a bead every other stitch, alternating yellow and aqua beads.

Completed!

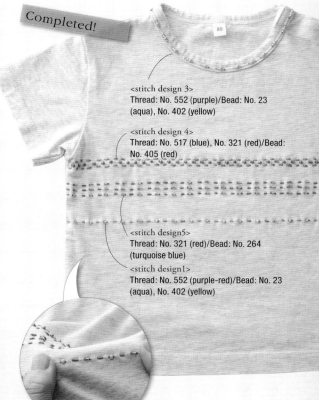

<stitch design 3>
Thread: No. 552 (purple)/Bead: No. 23 (aqua), No. 402 (yellow)

<stitch design 4>
Thread: No. 517 (blue), No. 321 (red)/Bead: No. 405 (red)

<stitch design5>
Thread: No. 321 (red)/Bead: No. 264 (turquoise blue)

<stitch design1>
Thread: No. 552 (purple-red)/Bead: No. 23 (aqua), No. 402 (yellow)

When you stitch on stretchy fabric such as a T-shirt, stretch the work slightly before making a knot so that the thread isn't too loose or tight.

1
Make a leaf using the Lazy Daisy stitch. Make the right leaf in the same way.

2 Pull the needle out of the leaf base, make straight stitches as a stem, then pull the needle out of the fabric a bit forward.

3 Thread a magatama bead, then insert the needle into the fabric alongside the stem, returning a bit. Repeat this for the right stem.

Completed!

Running Stitches

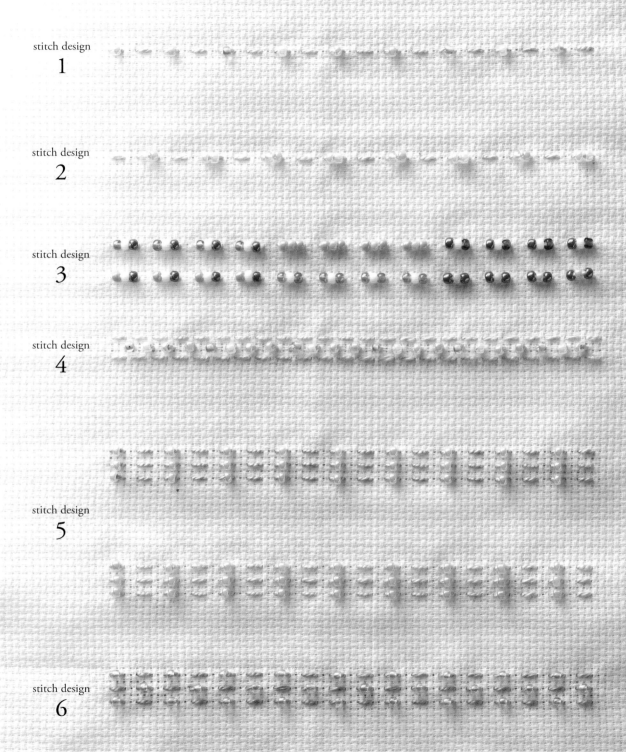

stitch design
1

stitch design
2

stitch design
3

stitch design
4

stitch design
5

stitch design
6

Adding beads to running stitches

Running Stitch
Make a few stitches at a time, passing the needle in and out of the fabric. This is the most basic stitch.

How to make running stitces

1 Insert a bead every other stitch. When you use various colors, make sure the tone is uniform.

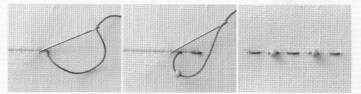

2 Insert two beads every other stitch. You can enjoy various expressions with a combination of colors.

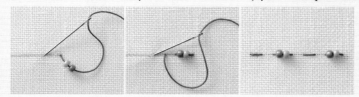

3 Insert three beads every stitch. Make one stitch a little longer than the width of three beads.

4 Work running stitches in between two rows of stitches, inserting a bead every stitch and staggering the needle inseration point.

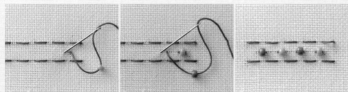

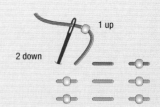

5 Make three rows of the stitch shown in 1, properly aligning the position. Beads of the same color look lovely.

6 Stitches shown in 1 with staggered positions.

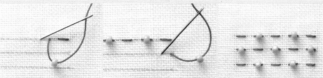
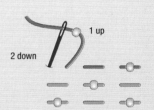

Running Stitches (1-6)

Straight Stitches
Back/Pekinese Stitches
Outline/Holbein Stitches
Branket/Buttonhole Stitches

LESSON-1

Dress on the left page: Collar & hem <stitch design 13> DMC #5/3689 (pink)/round bead 8/0 (3.0mm) No.905 (pink), No.901 (yellow), No.919 (blue), No.943 (purple), No.173 (lime green) / Waist <stitch design 14> DMC #5/3689 (pink)/round bead 8/0 (3.0mm) No.905 (pink), No.919 (blue), No.901 (yellow), <stitch design 23> DMC #5/3689 (pink)/round bead 8/0 (3.0mm) No.905 (pink), No.919 (blue), No.901 (yellow), No.943 (purple), No.173 (lime green)

Baby shoes: <stitch design 11> DMC #5/164 (grass green)/round bead 8/0 (3.0mm) No.405 (red), / Cherry (page 14) DMC #5/164 (grass green)/magatama bead M25 4mm, 1/8" (red)

Baby camisole & panty: neckline <stitch design 32> DMC #5/164 (grass green)/round bead 8/0 (3.0mm) No.905 (pink), No.901 (yellow), No.919 (blue), No.943 (purple), No.105 (lime green) / Chest <stitch design 11> DMC #5/164 (grass green)/round bead 8/0 (3.0mm) No.405 (red) / Cherry (page 14) DMC #5/164 (grass green)/ magatama bead M25 4mm, 1/8" (red)

19

Straight Stitches

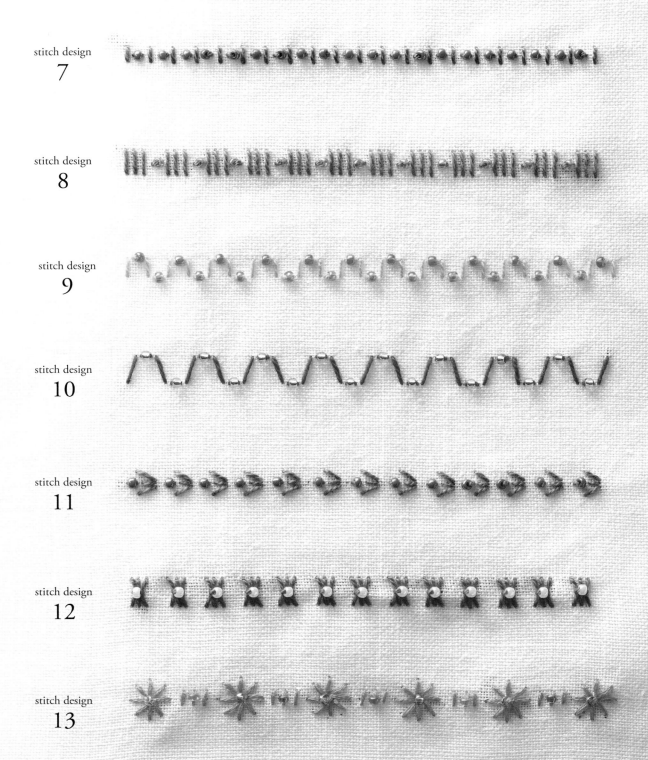

stitch design
7

stitch design
8

stitch design
9

stitch design
10

stitch design
11

stitch design
12

stitch design
13

Adding beads to a straight stitch

7   Insert a bead in between straight stitches.

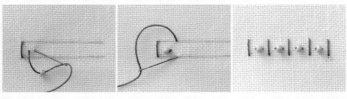

Straight Stitch

This is a basic stitch to form a straight line. You can make various patterns by stitching lines in parallel or in a radial fashion, varying the length and direction.

8   Insert a bead every four straight stitches. <Raft>

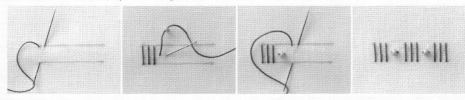

9   Make a straight stitch and insert a bead, then repeat the steps for the opposite side. <Bump>

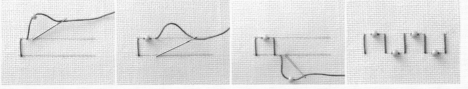

10   Make straight stitches at an angle, inserting a bead in between stitches. <Zigzag>

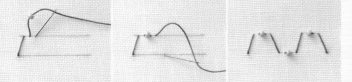

11   Turn straight stitches as stems and leaves. <Flowery border>

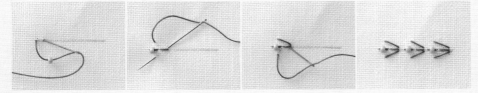

12   Collect three straight stitches with a bead. <Firewood>

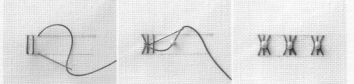

13   Make the straight stitches in a radial fashion, and insert a bead in the center. <Sunflower>

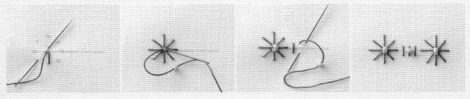

Straight Stitches (7-13)

LESSON-1

Back/Pekinese Stitches

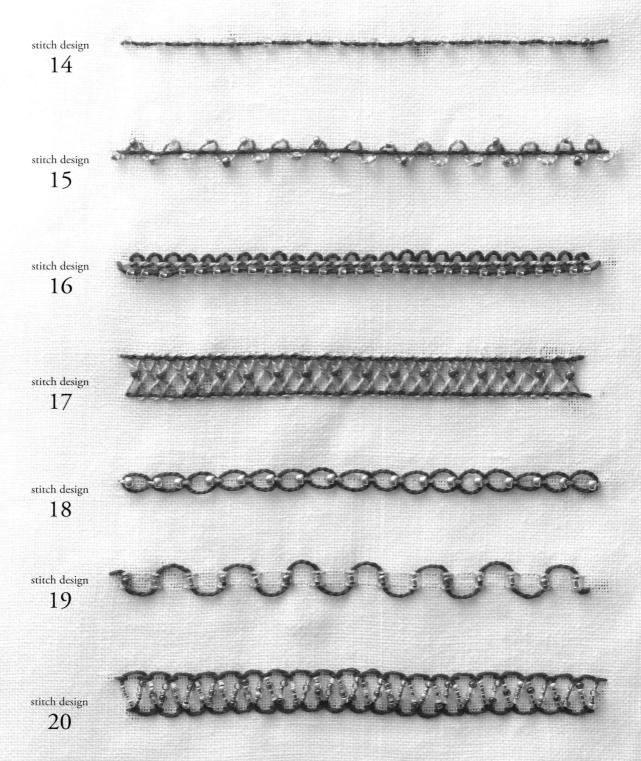

stitch design
14

stitch design
15

stitch design
16

stitch design
17

stitch design
18

stitch design
19

stitch design
20

Adding beads to back/Pekinese stitches

14 Insert a bead every other stitch in the basic back stitches.

<table>
<tr><td>

Back Stitch

This stitch is often used to make an outline, stitching backwards and proceeding from right to left. Try to make the width of the stitches uniform.

</td><td>

Pekinese Stitch

Chinese traditional stitch. Loop a thread around the base of back stitches, and a beautiful shaded stitch is formed, like an embroidered blade.

</td></tr>
</table>

15 Insert a bead every other stitch in threaded back stitches. <Wave>

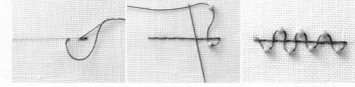

16 Using the back stitches as a base, make loops with other thread inserting beads. <Pekinese stitch>

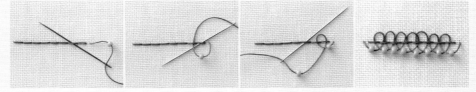

17 Make loops on two lines of back stitches like hairpin lace. <Double Pekinese stitch>

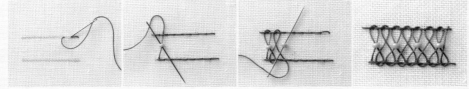

18 Make running stitches with beads and pass other thread through the stitches. <Threaded running stitch>

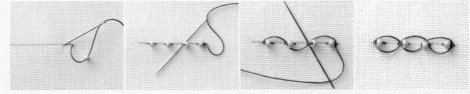

19 Make two rows of running stitch, and pass other thread through the stitches, inserting beads in between the two rows.

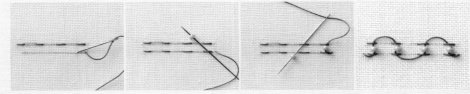

20 Make two rows of running stitch, and pass other thread through the stitches, inserting four beads at a time in between the two rows.

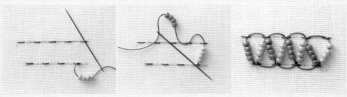

Back/Pekinese Stitches (14-20)

Outline/Holbein Stitches

stitch design
21

stitch design
22

stitch design
23

stitch design
24

stitch design
25

stitch design
26

stitch design
27

Adding beads to outline/Holbein stitches

21 Insert a bead every other stitch in outline stitches.

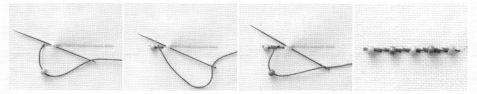

Outline Stitch

This stitch is used for outlining straight and curved lines. Stitch back stitches from left to right at an angle, and pull the needle out of the fabric in the middle of the stitch you are creating. Try to stitch uniformly.

Holbein Stitch

The name comes from embroidery drawn in a painting by a German artist Hans Holbein. It looks the same on both the front and back, and is suited for complex geometric patterns and delicate outlines.

LESSON-1

22 Stitch outline stitches the width of two beads, making the stitches overlap considerably.

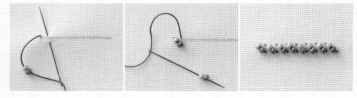

23 Stitch angular outline stitches which are symmetrical about the top and bottom. <Arrow stitch>

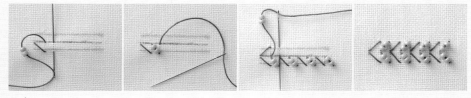

24 Stitch running stitches with beads, and fill in the gaps with other thread. <Holbein stitch>

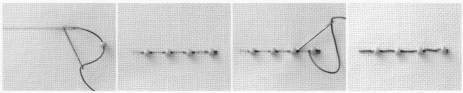

25 Stitch Holbein stitches to make a bump pattern, and add beads one by one in the gaps.

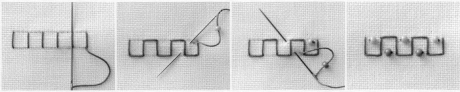

26 Stitch zigzag to make a chevron pattern, and add beads one by one on the corner.

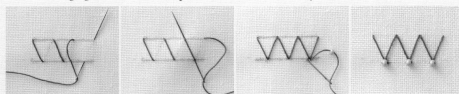

27 Stitch zigzag and add beads one by one in the gaps with running stitches.

Outline/Holbein Stitches (21-27)

Blanket/Buttonhole Stitches

stitch design
28

stitch design
29

stitch design
30

stitch design
31

stitch design
32

stitch design
33

stitch design
34

Adding beads to blanket/buttonhole stitches

28 Stitch buttonhole stitches symmetrically about the top and bottom, and add beads one by one in the middle.

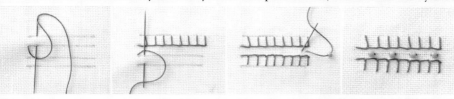

29 ???

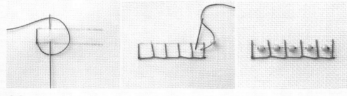

30 Insert a bead every other stitch in the buttonhole stitches.

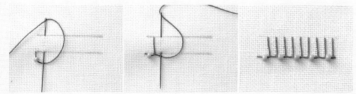

31 Insert a bead every other stitch in the blanket stitches with a shorter length.

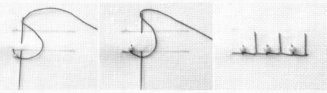

32 Insert long and short bugle beads and small round beads to make a flower field pattern.

33 Stitch blanket stitches, running the needle diagonally to form triangles, and add beads in the center. <Closed buttonhole stitch>

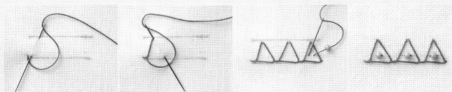

34 Wrap the thread over the needle twice in stitching buttonhole stitches. It looks like the ears of a running and jumping rabbit.

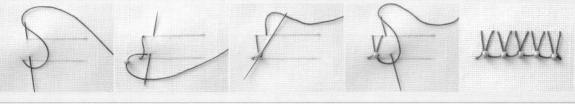

LESSON-1

Lazy Daisy Stitches
Chain Stitches, Closs Stitches
Chevron/Herringbone Stitches
Fern/Fly Stitches, Couching Stitches
Opeen Cretan Stitches
Zigzag Stitches, Feather Stitches

LESSON-2

Stole on the left page: <stitch design 43> Appleton 758 (dark pink) / round bead 8/0 (3.0mm) 332 (red-purple), <stitch design36> Appleton 144 (pink), 758 (dark pink) / round bead 8/0 (3.0mm) 332 (red-purple), <stitch design37> Appleton 758 (dark pink) / round bead 8/0 (3.0mm) 906 (pink), 332 (red-purple), <stitch design38> Appleton 544 (lime green) / round bead 8/0 (3.0mm) 122 (milk), 105 (lime green), <stitch design 38> Appleton 144 (pink) /round bead 8/0 (3.0mm) 906 (pink) & 106 (light pink)

Cardigan: <stitch design 54> DMC #25 304 (red, double yarn) / round bead 8/0 (3.0mm) 332 (red-purple), 559 (gold), <stitch design 93> Appleton 187 (brown) /round bead 8/0 (3.0mm) 332 (red-purple) & 559 (gold)

Socks: Left - <stitch design 67> Appleton 564 (blue) / round bead 8/0 (3.0mm) 23 (blue), 170 (pale blue), 264 (turquoise blue) / Right - <stitch design 67> Appleton 454 (purple) /round bead 8/0 (3.0mm) 977 (light purple), 170 (pale blue), 264 (turquoise blue)/ Common - <stitch design 61> Appleton 544 (green), 758 (red) / round bead 8/0 (3.0mm) 105 (lime green) * All yarn threads are doubled.

Lazy Daisy Stitches

stitch design
35

stitch design
36

stitch design
37

stitch design
38

stitch design
39

stitch design
40

stitch design
41

Adding beads to Lazy Daisy stitches

35 Fix the basic Lazy Daisy stitch with one bead.

> **Lazy Daisy Stitch**
>
> As the name implies, small petals are stitched radially to look like a pretty daisy. Stitch in the same way as a chain stitch.

36 Fix the Lazy Daisy stitch and pass other thread through the stitches. <Threaded chain stitch>

37 Insert two beads each time using a combination of the fly stitch and Lazy Daisy stitch.

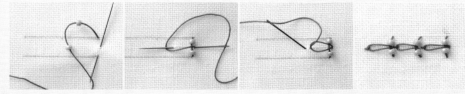

38 Stitch Lazy Daisy stitches symmetrically about the top and bottom to form cotyledon, or seed leaf, and add two beads in between the motifs.

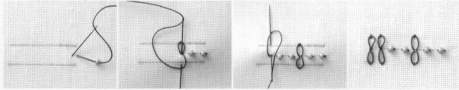

39 Link Lazy Daisy stitches with back stitch and a bead.

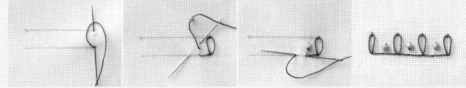

40 Stitch a combination of Lazy Daisy stitches and alternating beads up and down.

41 Stitch Lazy Daisy stitches fixed with a bead to form a cross. It looks like a pretty thread ball.

Lazy Daisy Stitches (35-41)

LESSON-2

Chain Stitches

stitch design
42

stitch design
43

stitch design
44

stitch design
45

stitch design
46

stitch design
47

stitch design
48

Adding beads to chain stitches

42   Stitch chain stitches, and add beads in the center with running stitches.

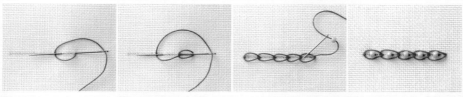

Chain Stitch

This stitch is made by linking small loops like a chain. It is one of the most traditional stitches and has been used in antique fabrics around the world.

43   Add beads one by one in cable chain stitches.

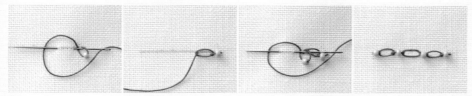

44   Stitch cable chain stitches in a zigzag manner, adding a bead each time.

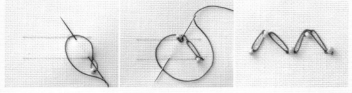

45   Fix chained feather stitches with two beads.

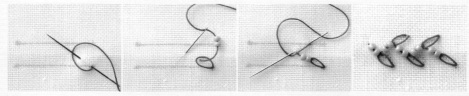

46   Add three beads every other stitch of the open chain stitches.

47   Collect three open chain stitches with a bead.

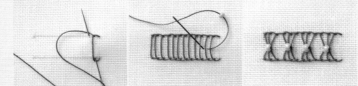

48   Add beads in crested chain stitches.

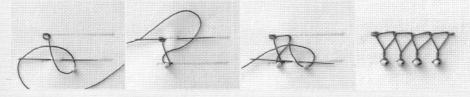

33

LESSON-2

stitch design
49

stitch design
50

stitch design
51

stitch design
52

stitch design
53

stitch design
54

stitch design
55

Adding beads to cross stitches

49 Insert beads one by one in between the basic cross stitches.

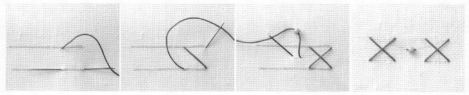

50 Insert a bead into the center of the basic cross stitch, and link the crosses with straight stitches.

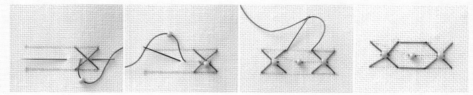

51 Insert a bead into the center of a rice stitch (raised knot).

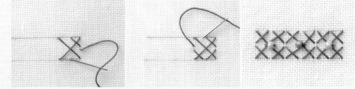

52 Insert a bead into the center of a star filling stitch, and link the stitches that have running stitches with beads.

53 Combine cross stitches with beads in the center.

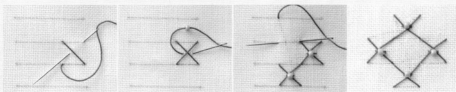

54 Stitch cross stitches with two beads on each line to make flower motifs.

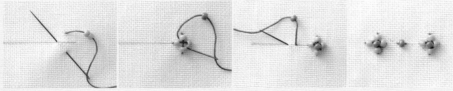

55 Insert a bead into the cross, twisting the thread around the center.

Cross Stitches (49-55)

LESSON-2

Chevron/Herringbone Stitches

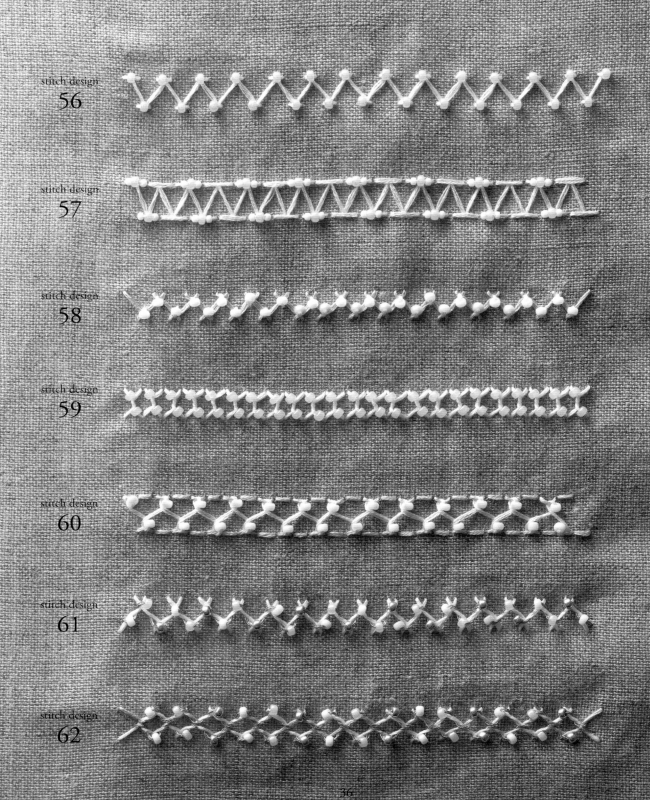

stitch design
56

stitch design
57

stitch design
58

stitch design
59

stitch design
60

stitch design
61

stitch design
62

Adding beads to chevron & herringbone stitches

56 Add beads one by one in chevron stitches.

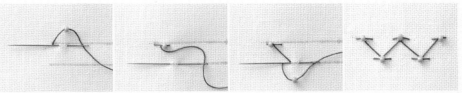

57 Add three beads at a time in chevron stitches.

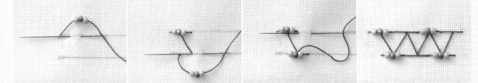

58 Add a bead to the cross point of a herringbone stitch.

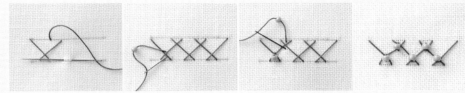

59 Add beads one by one in twisted herringbone stitches.

60 Add beads one by one with other thread to back stitches. <Herringbone ladder filling stitch>

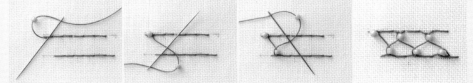

61 Pass other thread with beads through herringbone stitches. <Threaded herringbone stitch>

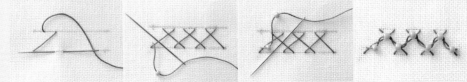

62 Pass other thread with beads through double herringbone stitches. <Twisted lattice band>

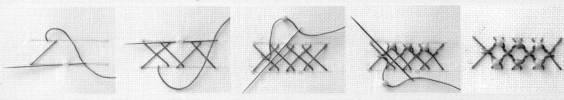

Chevron Stitch

This stitch is worked making back stitches from left to right in a zigzag manner. Draw parallel lines with a water-soluble marker before stitching to create a beautiful finish.

Herringbone Stitch

This is a border stitch to make crossed zigzags look like the "bones of a herring". You can arrange the stitch in various ways, for example passing other thread through the stitches. It is called "Chidorigake (catch stitch)" in Japanese dressmaking.

LESSON-2

Fern/Fly Stitches

stitch design
63

stitch design
64

stitch design
65

stitch design
66

stitch design
67

stitch design
68

stitch design
69

Adding beads to fern/fly stitches

63 Add beads one by one to the center of the basic fern stitch.

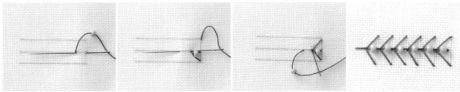

64 Add beads to fern stitches to make a flowery border.

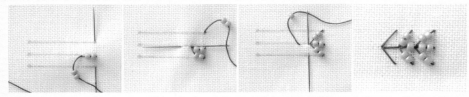

Fern Stitch

This stitch is widely branched and is reminiscent of fern fronds. Draw three parallel lines using a water-soluble marker to make balanced stitches. You can make various motifs depending on the bead placement.

Fly Stitch

Beginners can arrange the stitch, anyway they like, for example linking the stitches in any direction to draw stripes, or making stitches of different lengths. Make several fly stitches in a row and you can form feather stitches.

65 Make fly stitches, increasing the number of beads to form a tree.

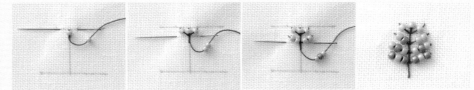

66 Add beads to the basic fly stitches.

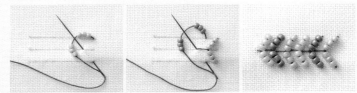

67 Stitch fly stitches symmetrically along the top and bottom, adding two beads at a time, and accent them with beads in the center.

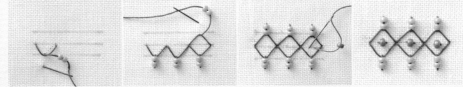

68 Stitch small and large fly stitches which are opposite one another, adding beads. <Reversed fly stitch>

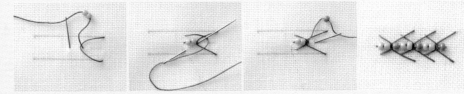

69 Split beads symmetrically and fix them with a long stitch. <Bull's horn stitch>

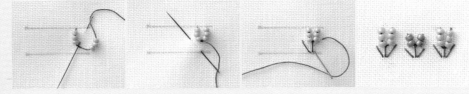

LESSON-2

39

Fern/Fly Stitches (63-69)

Couching Stitches

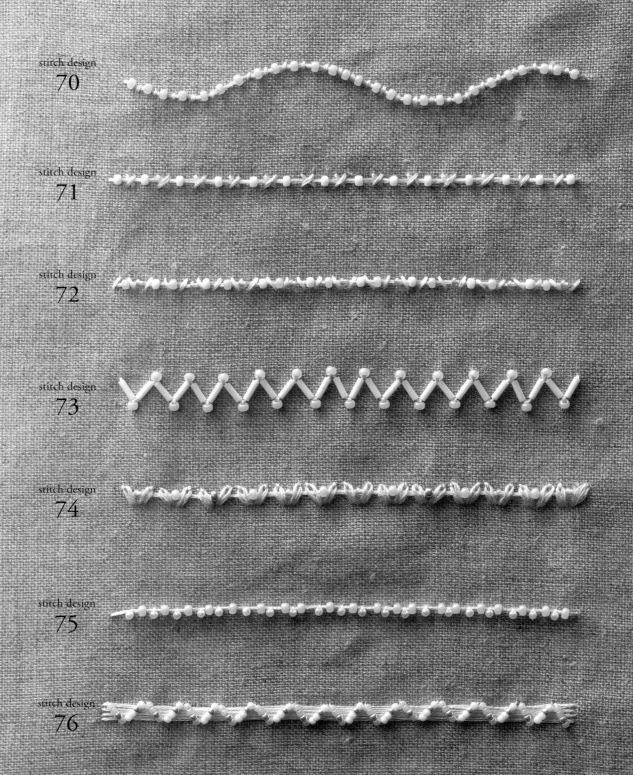

stitch design
70

stitch design
71

stitch design
72

stitch design
73

stitch design
74

stitch design
75

stitch design
76

Adding beads to couching stitches

70 Add beads to the thread to be laid in the basic couching stitch.

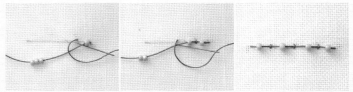

Couching Stitch

The name derives from the French word "coucher (lay)." Lay a thread on top of a fabric and stitch with another supple thread to hold the first thread in place. With this stitch, you can use thick thread or gold thread for finely woven fabric.

71 Fix a beaded thread by cross stitches.

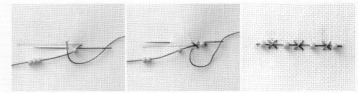

72 Fix a beaded thread in a fun zigzag manner.

73 Fix a thread beaded with bugle beads in a zigzag manner, adding round beads 8/0.(3.0mm).

74 Fix a thread beaded with round beads 8/0(3.0mm) by Lazy Daisy stitches.

75 Fix a thread beaded with round beads 11/0 (2.2mm) with round beads 11/0 (2.2mm).

76 Layer embroidery thread and fix four beads at a time in a zigzag manner. <Fancy couching stitch>

Couching Stitches (70-76)

LESSON-2

Open Cretan Stitches

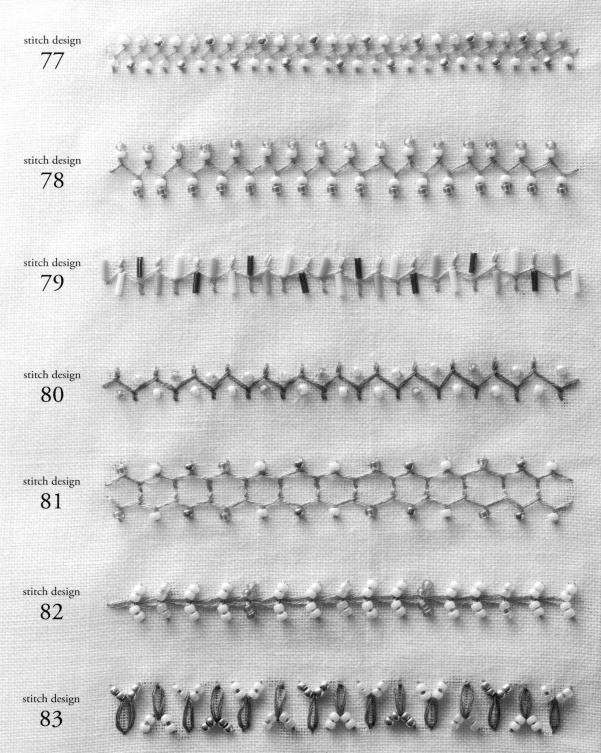

stitch design
77

stitch design
78

stitch design
79

stitch design
80

stitch design
81

stitch design
82

stitch design
83

Adding beads to open Cretan stitches

77 Insert beads one by one into Cretan stitches.

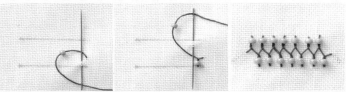

> **Open Cretan Stitch**
> This stitch was commonly used for decoration of linen and clothes in Cretan hence its name. Stitch it at intervals to make an open Cretan stitch.

78 Insert two beads at a time into open Cretan stitches.

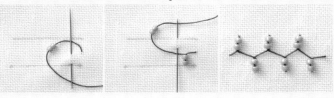

79 Add bugle beads in between open Cretan stitches.

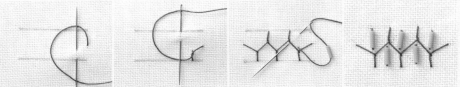

80 Insert beads one by one in between open Cretan stitches.

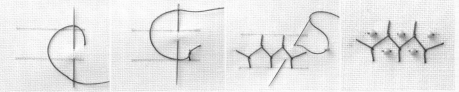

81 Stitch open Cretan stitches symmetrically about the top and bottom to form geometric patterns.

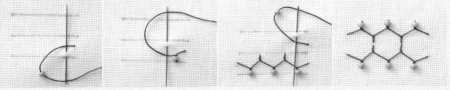

82 Insert two beads at a time into Wheatear stitches.

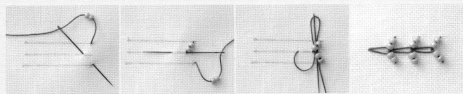

83 Fix fly stitches that have beads with Lazy Daisy stitches. <Fly & Lazy Daisy stitch>

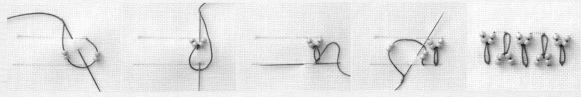

Open Cretan Stitches (77-83)

LESSON-2

Zigzag Stitches

stitch design
84

stitch design
85

stitch design
86

stitch design
87

stitch design
88

stitch design
89

stitch design
90

Adding beads to zigzag stitches

84 Make the basic zigzag stitches adding round beads 8/0(3.0mm) and bugle beads.

85 Make two rows of paralles zigzag stitches and add beads one by one in between the rows.

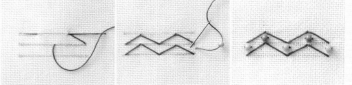

86 Stitch zigzag stitches symmetrically along the top and bottom, adding round beads 8/0(3.0mm) one by one to the center.

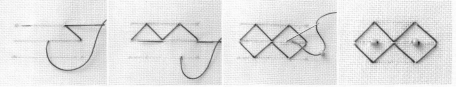

87 Make two rows of altered zigzag stitches and add bugle beads and round beads in between the rows.

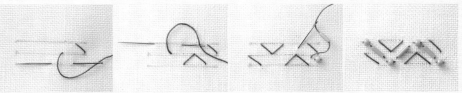

88 Stitch altered zigzag stitches almost overlapping with each other, adding bugle beads one by one.

89 Add four beads at a time in altered zigzag stitches. Fix the crossed center with a stitch.

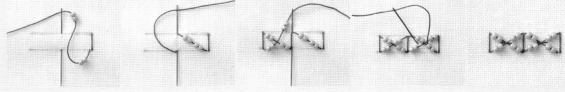

90 Add two beads at a time in altered zigzag stitches in the shape of arrows. <Arrow stitch>

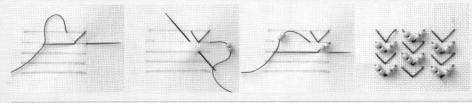

Zigzag Stitches (84-90)

LESSON·2

Feather Stitches

with Beads

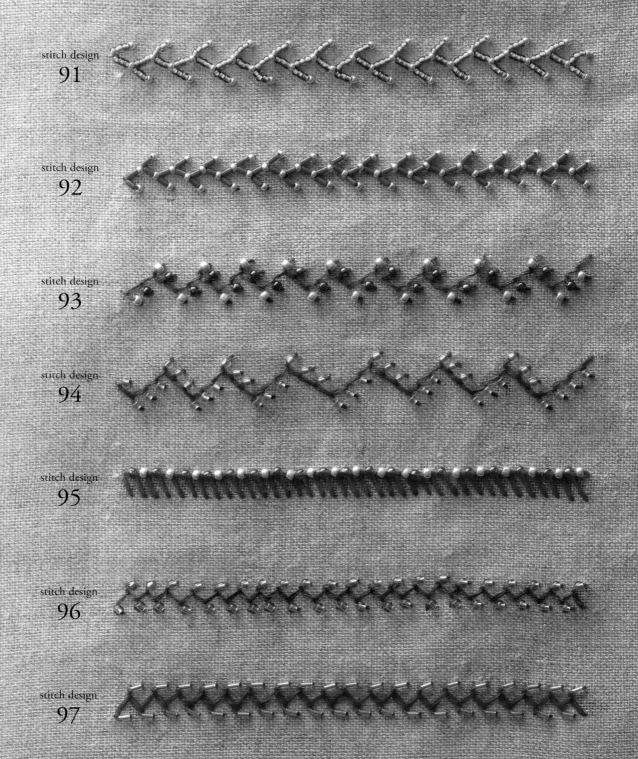

stitch design
91

stitch design
92

stitch design
93

stitch design
94

stitch design
95

stitch design
96

stitch design
97

Adding beads to feather stitches

How to stitch ▶ P.78

91 Insert eight beads at a time in feather stitches. Split the beads with a fixing stitch.

92 Insert round beads 8/0.(3.0mm) and bugle beads in feather stitches to make coral patterns .

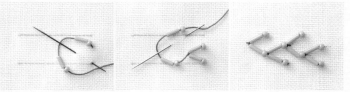

Feather Stitch

This stitch is made by alternately stitching rows, resembling airy feathers. It is the application of fly stitches and is also called the single coral stitch.

93 Add beads one by one in double feather stitches. They look like small currants.

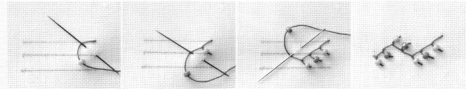

94 Add beads one by one in double feather stitches, increasing the number of stitches to widen it.

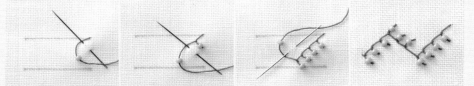

95 Add beads one by one in single feather stitches, extending one side.

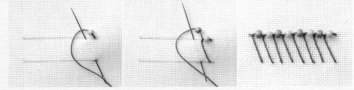

96 Add beads one by one in altered feather stitches.

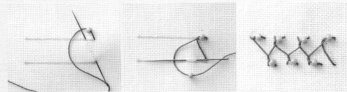

97 Add bugle beads one by one in altered feather stitches.

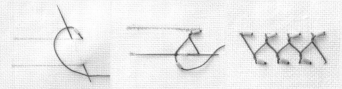

Feather Stitches with Beads (91-97)

Lace Motif
Edging Stitches
Filling Stitches
One Point Motif

LESSON-3

Parasol on the left page:<application of stitch design 111> DMC #25/838 (dark brown, double yarn), No.3790 (beige)/ round bead 8/0.(3.0mm) No.22 (gold), round bead 11/0 (2.2mm) No.401 (white), No.22 (gold)
* All yarn threads are doubled.

Linen dress: <application of stitch design 111> DMC #12/B5200 (white)/ round bead 8/0 (3.0mm) No.401 (white)/ round bead 11/0 (2.2mm) No.401 (white), No.21 (silver) <stitch design 110> DMC #12/B5200 (white)/ round bead 11/0 (2.2mm) No.401 (white)

Handkerchiefs: Gingham <stitch design 116> DMC #25/842 (beige, triple yarn) / round bead 11/0 (2.2mm) No.105 (lime green), No.174 (orange), No.332 (red purple), No.402 (yellow), No.125 (red) / White linen: <stitch design 112> DMC #25/304 (red, triple yarn)/ round bead 8/0 (3.0mm) No.22 (gold), No.105 (lime green) No.165 (red) / Linen <stitch design 118> DMC #25/304 (red, quadruple yarn)/ round bead 8/0 (3.0mm) No.122 (milk), No.125 (red)

Lace Motifs

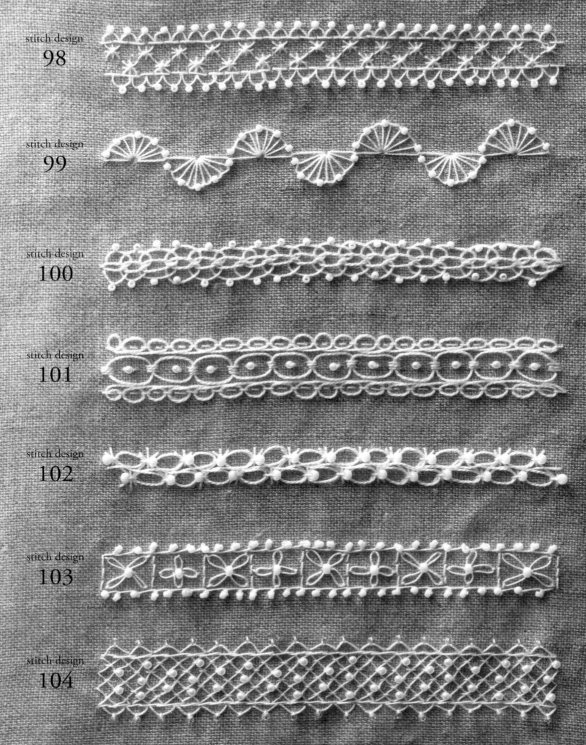

stitch design
98

stitch design
99

stitch design
100

stitch design
101

stitch design
102

stitch design
103

stitch design
104

Adding beads to white lace motifs

98   Add scallop motifs with beads to star filling stitches.

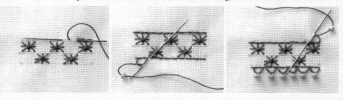

Lace Motif

A neat lace motif consisting of several stitches transforms a collection of simple stitches into a delicate and complex motif by layering simple stitches or passing other threads through the stitches.

99   A fan motif of buttonhole stitches with alternating beads.

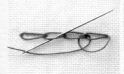 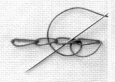  

100   Make chain stitches, pass other thread through both sides of the stitches and fix them with beads. <Interlaced chain design>

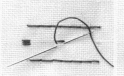 

101   Pass other thread through the basic stitches to make lace motifs such as ribbons. <Guilloche stitch>

  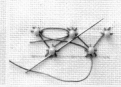

102   Combine star filling stitches to make a constellation-like motif. <Fancy herringbone stitch>

 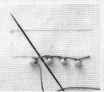 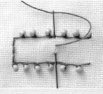 

103   Make rosette chain stitches with beads and Lazy Daisy stitches to make motifs such as Tyrolean tape.

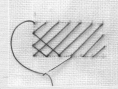 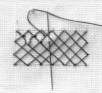

104   Make bead flowers on trellis couching stitches.

Lace Motif (98-104)

Lace Motifs

stitch design
105

stitch design
106

stitch design
107

stitch design
108

stitch design
109

stitch design
110

stitch design
111

Adding beads to white lace motifs

105 Using zigzag stitches as a guide, make elongated Lazy Daisy stitches.

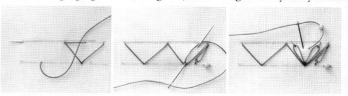

106 Add scallop motifs of crested chain stitches to a border of flowers consisting of Lazy Daisy stitches and bugle beads.

107 Fix the loops of Maltese stitches with fly stitches and beads.

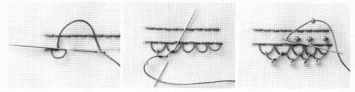

108 Add Lazy Daisy stitches in a radial fashion to make gorgeous motifs like water lilies.

109 Make three-dimensional lace motifs with twisted zigzag chain stitches and bead flowers.

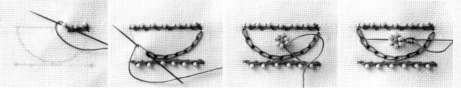

110 Make back stitches in a regular manner to make a border of symbolic roses.

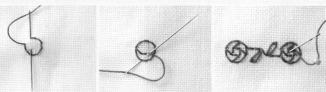

111 Make wide lace with cross stitches and add fringes of beads and Lazy Daisy stitches to produce a rhythmical mood.

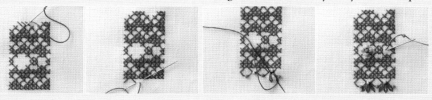

LESSON-3

Lace Motifs (105-111)

Edging Stitches

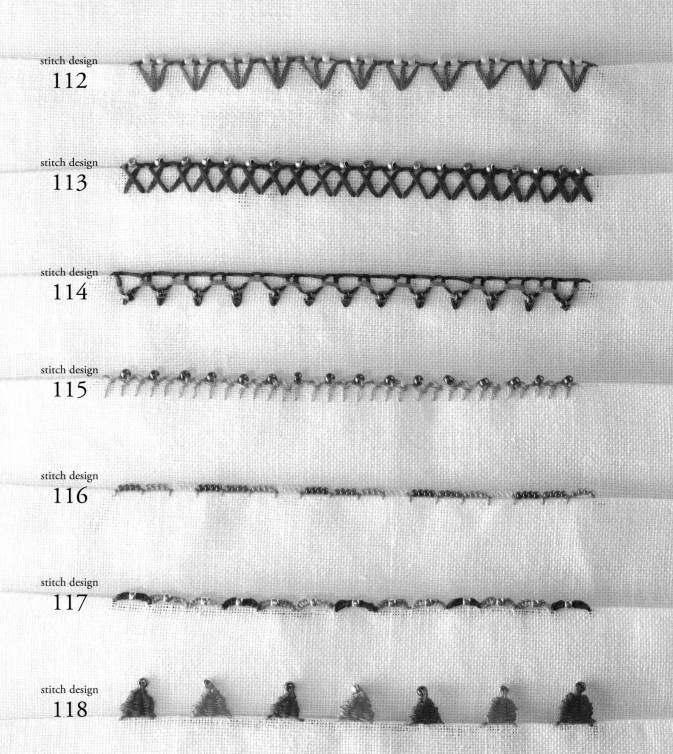

stitch design
112

stitch design
113

stitch design
114

stitch design
115

stitch design
116

stitch design
117

stitch design
118

Adding beads to edging stitches

112 Add beads to elongated closed buttonhole stitches to accentuate the edge.

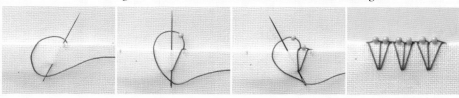

Edging Stitch

Edging stitches on sleeve edges or hems will transform your clothing into your own one-of-a-kind items. There are countless combinations of bead and thread. It also works well on pieces such as handkerchiefs or bags.

113 Add beads to crossed buttonhole stitches.

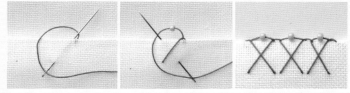

114 Pass a beaded thread through closed buttonhole stitches.

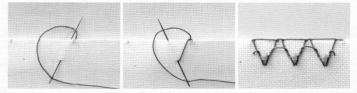

115 Add beads to buttonhole chain edging stitches.

116 Add four beads at a time in Armenian edging stitches.

117 Make buttonhole stitches using to-and-from threads as the core. The picot of one bead looks cute.

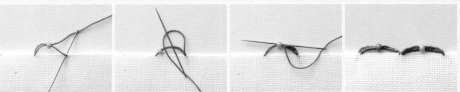

118 Make three-dimensional uvan picots using a loop of core thread as warp thread.
Tighten the thread of the first three or four stitches to make a pointed triangle.

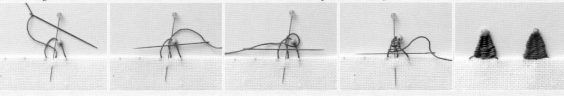

LESSON-3

Edging Stitches (112-118)

Filling Stitches

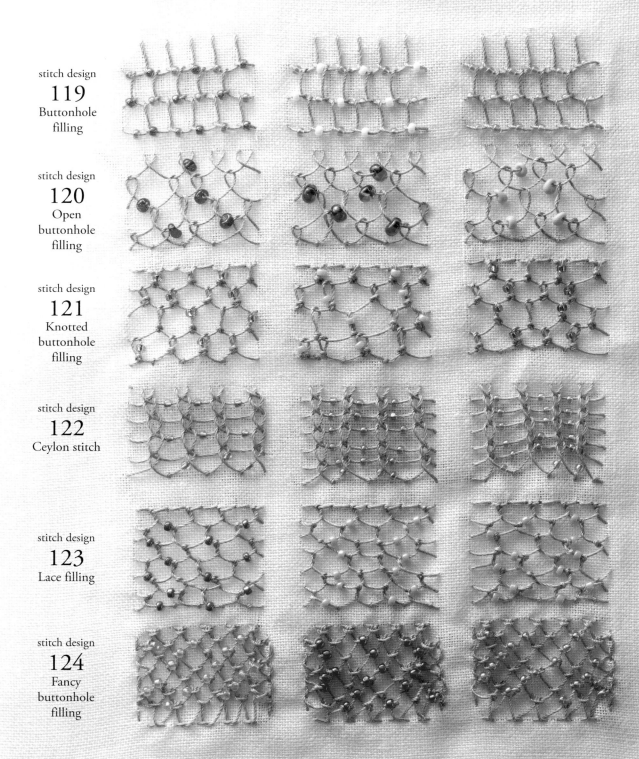

stitch design
119
Buttonhole
filling

stitch design
120
Open
buttonhole
filling

stitch design
121
Knotted
buttonhole
filling

stitch design
122
Ceylon stitch

stitch design
123
Lace filling

stitch design
124
Fancy
buttonhole
filling

Adding beads to filling stitches

LESSON-3

Filling Stitch

This is used to fill in the surface. It is mainly formed by passing the thread through the stitches or loops and the texture can be enjoyed like a knit. It looks different depending on the beads used.

T-shirt: <stitch design 120> hemp yarn (ramie), medium-thin sewing thread (natural)/ magatama bead (5mm, 1/5") No. M248 (blue), magatama bead (4mm, 1/8") No. M07 (green), No. M01 (clear), round bead 8/0 (3.0mm) No. 23 (aqua), No. 21 (silver)

120 Make loops in the same way as back stitches, then pass the thread through the loops taking only the thread (not the fabric) and adding beads.

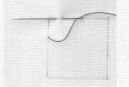 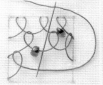

Filling Stitches (119-124)

One Point Motifs

stitch design
125

stitch design
126

stitch design
127

stitch design
128

stitch design
129

stitch design
130

One point motifs that make beads or spangles stand out

One Point Motif

The same motif dramatically changes if you change the combination of thread and beads. Use a marker to make a beautiful motif.

Camisole: <stitch design 129> hexagonal spangle (5mm, 1/5") No. 502 (green), 6mm-long bugle bead No. 27 (green), 3mm-long bugle bead No. 27 (green), round bead 11/0 (2.2mm) No. 557 (gold), <stitch design 129> hexagonal spangle (5mm, 1/5") No. 504 (blue), 6mm-long bugle bead No. 23 (blue), 3mm-long bugle bead No. 23 (blue), round bead 11/0 (2.2mm) No. 557 (gold), <stitch design 130> hexagonal spangle (5mm, 1/5") No. 502 (green), No. 504 (blue), 3mm-long bugle bead No. 22 (gold), round bead 11/0 (2.2mm) No. 557 (gold) *The sewing yarn #60 (white, double yarn) is used for all.

128 Flower motif of Lazy Daisy stitch which looks different, depending on the length of bugle beads

 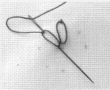 

One Point Motif (125-130)

Alphabet A to Z

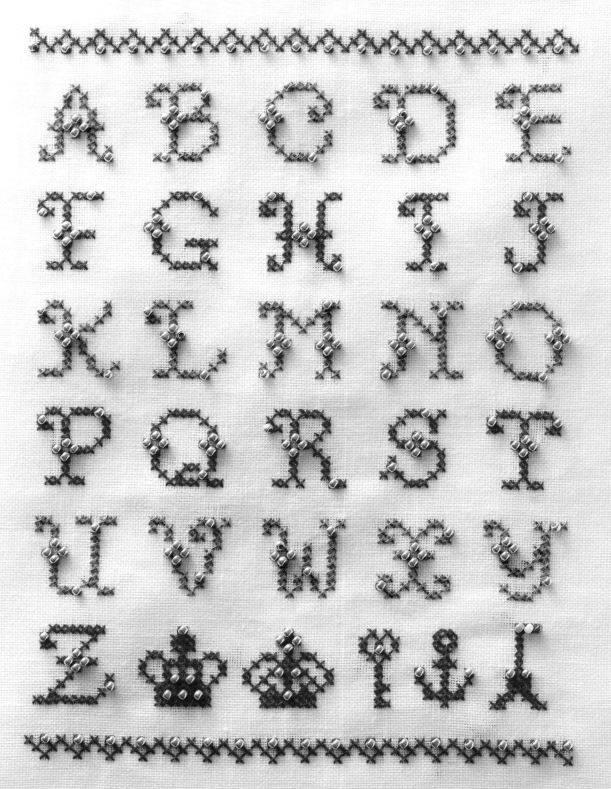

Alphabet A to Z with Beads
Nordic Motifs with Beads

DESIGN CHARTS

Sneakers: DMC #25/597 (saxe blue, quadruple yarn)/ round bead 8/0 (3.0mm) No. 23 (aqua), No. 21 (silver)

For the stitches for the sneakers and canvas backpack, DMC's original alphabet stamps (see page 7) were used. For the positioning of beads, please refer to page 64.

Canvas backpack: DMC #25/517 (blue, quadruple yarn)/ round bead 8/0 (3.0mm) No. 401 (white), No. 405 (red), <stitch design 1 & 5> DMC #25/311 (dark blue, quadruple yarn)/round bead 8/0 (3.0mm) No. 401 (white)

61

Nordic Motifs

Cross stitch charts of Nordic motifs

#25 embroidery thread (double yarn)

■	No. 3838 (deep marine blue)	■	No. 322 (deep saxe blue)
■	No. 3839 (marine blue)	■	No. 3755 (saxe blue)
■	No. 3840 (pale marine blue)	■	No. 3841 (pale saxe blue)

Round bead 8/0 (3.0mm)
◯ Add beads of No. 559 (platinum) while cross stitching.

◯ Add beads of No. 559 (platinum) with sewing yarn #60 (white, double yarn) after cross stitching.

Nordic Motif
You can use these motifs in as a sampler or even for borders or eye-catching motifs. Cool tones of blue are used here and platinum beads add a touch of gorgeousness.

Alphabet cross stitch charts

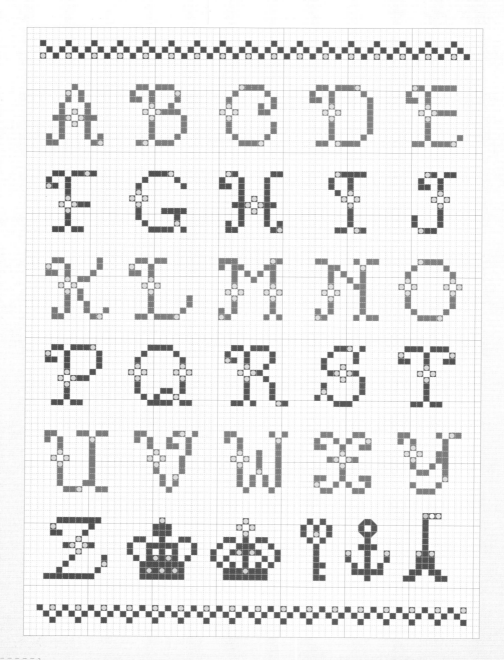

Alphabet

Add beads to a simple pattern which can be easily stitched to spice it up a bit. Enjoy variations by changing the type of thread, color of bead and size of stitch.

*For the cross stitch, please refer to page 10-11.

#25 embroidery thread (double yarn)
- ■ No. 347 (red)   ■ No. 931 (blue)

Round bead 8/0 (3.0mm)
Add beads while cross stitching. (See page 10)
- ○ No. 559 (platinum)   ○ No. 122 (white)
- ○ No. 403 (aqua)   ○ No. 405 (red)

Three quarter stitch

By changing the stitch length, you can make finer changes such as making corners round.

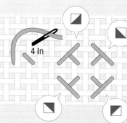

How to Stitch with Beads

This section shows how to make beaded embroidery stitches using illustrations in an easy-to-follow format. Gather needles, thread, fabric and your favorites beads, and let's get started!

For the type and number of embroidery threads, and size of well-matched beads, see the table below.

Threads and beads used for each sampler are listed on the last page of this book.

Recommended combination of needles, threads and beads

The following table shows needles suited for given threads and beads. But if you already have needles suitable for the threads and beads you need, go ahead and use them.
Basically embroidery needles are used, but for stretchy knit fabrics in long-sleeved shirts, T-shirts and the like, a ball-point needle for knits or jersey is recommended.

Needle		Thread	Bead
Embroidery needle	No.9	Embroidery thread No.25 (double and triple yarns)	Round bead 11/0 (2.2mm)/bugle bead
	No.8	Embroidery thread No.25 (triple-quadruple yarns), No.12 & No.8	Round bead 11/0 (2.2mm)/bugle bead
	No.7	Embroidery thread No.25 (double-quadruple yarns), No.8 & No.5	Round bead 8/0 (3.0mm)
	No.6	Embroidery thread No.25 (triple-quadruple yarns), No.5, cruel wool & hemp yarn	Round bead 8/0 (3.0mm)/magatama bead
Embroidery needle with blunt point	0.53mm	Embroidery thread No.25 (double yarn)	Round bead 11/0 (2.2mm)
	0.69mm	Embroidery thread No.25 (double-quadruple yarns) & No.12	Round bead 11/0 (2.2mm)
	0.84mm	Embroidery thread No.25 (quadruple yarn), No.12, No.8 & No.5	Round bead 8/0 (3.0mm)
Cross-stitch needle	No.23	Embroidery thread No.25 (double-triple yarns)	Round bead 8/0 (3.0mm)
	No.22	Embroidery thread No.25 (triple-quadruple yarns)	Round bead 8/0 (3.0mm)
Beads embroidery needle/sewing needle		Sewing yarn	Round bead 11/0 (2.2mm)/round bead 8/0 (3.0mm)/spangle

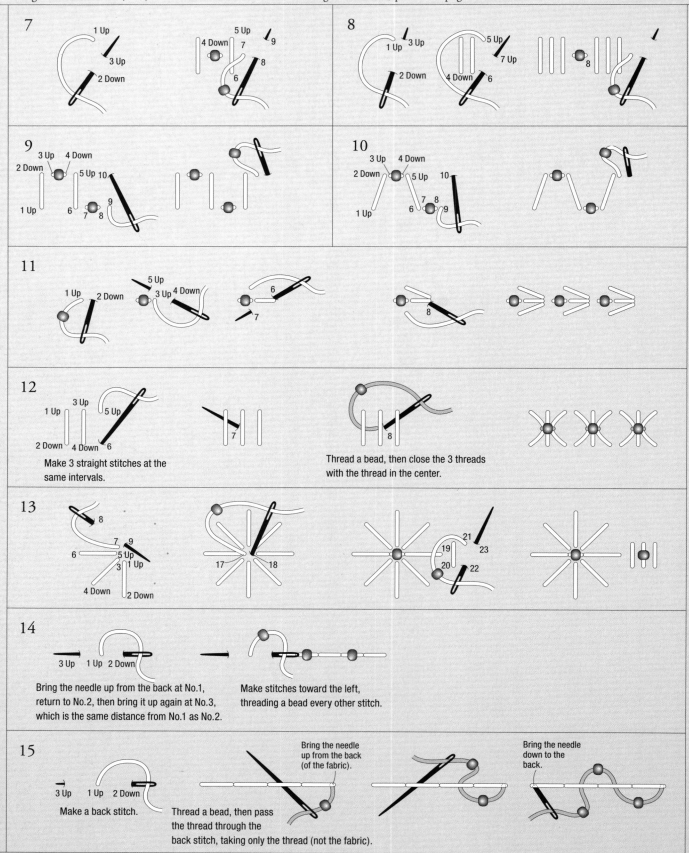

7

1 Up
3 Up
2 Down
5 Up
4 Down
7
6
8
9

8

1 Up
3 Up
2 Down
5 Up
4 Down
6
7 Up
8

9

3 Up 4 Down
2 Down
1 Up
5 Up 10
6
7 8
9

10

3 Up 4 Down
2 Down
1 Up
5 Up 10
6
7 8 9

11

1 Up
2 Down
5 Up
3 Up 4 Down
6
7
8

12

1 Up
3 Up
5 Up
2 Down
4 Down 6
7
8

Make 3 straight stitches at the same intervals.

Thread a bead, then close the 3 threads with the thread in the center.

13

8
7 9
6
5 Up
3 1 Up
4 Down 2 Down
17 18
19 21
20 23
22

14

3 Up   1 Up 2 Down

Bring the needle up from the back at No.1, return to No.2, then bring it up again at No.3, which is the same distance from No.1 as No.2.

Make stitches toward the left, threading a bead every other stitch.

15

3 Up   1 Up 2 Down

Make a back stitch.

Bring the needle up from the back (of the fabric).

Thread a bead, then pass the thread through the back stitch, taking only the thread (not the fabric).

Bring the needle down to the back.

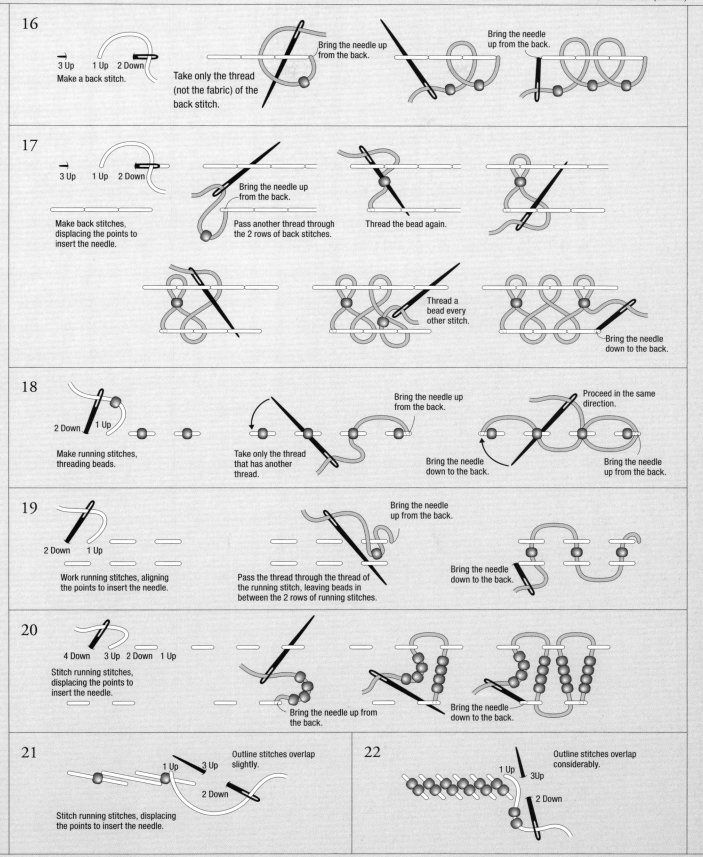

16

3 Up 1 Up 2 Down
Make a back stitch.

Take only the thread (not the fabric) of the back stitch.

Bring the needle up from the back.

Bring the needle up from the back.

17

3 Up 1 Up 2 Down

Make back stitches, displacing the points to insert the needle.

Bring the needle up from the back.
Pass another thread through the 2 rows of back stitches.

Thread the bead again.

Thread a bead every other stitch.

Bring the needle down to the back.

18

2 Down 1 Up

Make running stitches, threading beads.

Take only the thread that has another thread.

Bring the needle up from the back.
Bring the needle down to the back.

Proceed in the same direction.

Bring the needle up from the back.
Bring the needle down to the back.

19

2 Down 1 Up

Work running stitches, aligning the points to insert the needle.

Bring the needle up from the back.
Pass the thread through the thread of the running stitch, leaving beads in between the 2 rows of running stitches.

Bring the needle down to the back.

20

4 Down 3 Up 2 Down 1 Up

Stitch running stitches, displacing the points to insert the needle.

Bring the needle up from the back.

Bring the needle down to the back.

21

1 Up 3 Up
2 Down

Outline stitches overlap slightly.

Stitch running stitches, displacing the points to insert the needle.

22

1 Up 3Up
2 Down

Outline stitches overlap considerably.

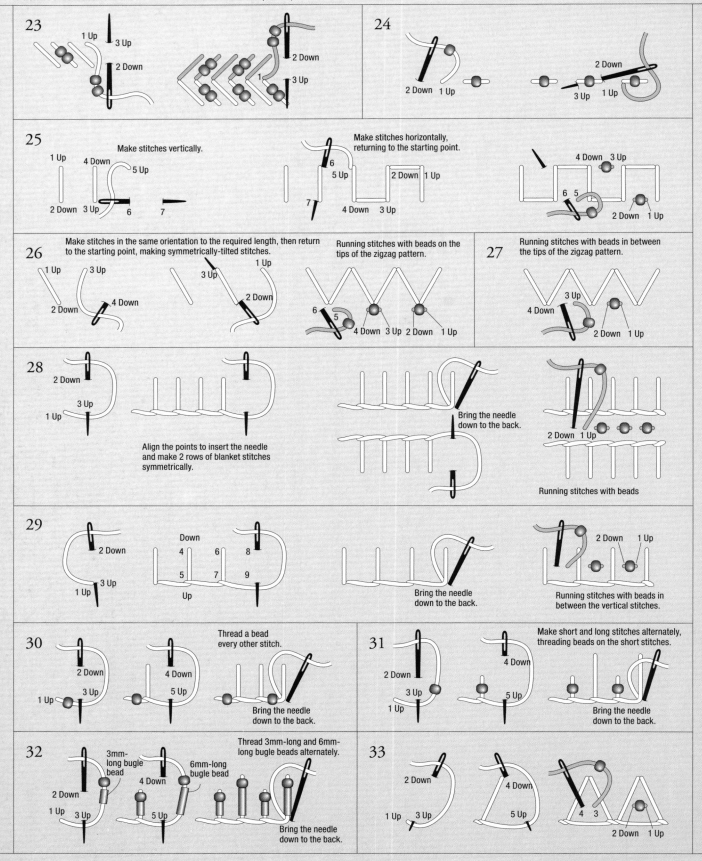

23

1 Up 3 Up 2 Down 2 Down 3 Up 1

24

2 Down 1 Up 3 Up 1 Up 2 Down

25

Make stitches vertically.

1 Up 4 Down 5 Up 2 Down 3 Up 6 7

Make stitches horizontally, returning to the starting point.

6 5 Up 2 Down 1 Up 7 4 Down 3 Up

4 Down 3 Up 6 5 2 Down 1 Up

26

Make stitches in the same orientation to the required length, then return to the starting point, making symmetrically-tilted stitches.

1 Up 3 Up 2 Down 4 Down 3 Up 2 Down 1 Up

Running stitches with beads on the tips of the zigzag pattern.

6 5 4 Down 3 Up 2 Down 1 Up

27

Running stitches with beads in between the tips of the zigzag pattern.

3 Up 4 Down 2 Down 1 Up

28

2 Down 3 Up 1 Up

Align the points to insert the needle and make 2 rows of blanket stitches symmetrically.

Bring the needle down to the back.

Bring the needle down to the back.

2 Down 1 Up

Running stitches with beads

29

2 Down 3 Up 1 Up

Down 4 6 8 5 7 9 Up

Bring the needle down to the back.

2 Down 1 Up

Running stitches with beads in between the vertical stitches.

30

Thread a bead every other stitch.

2 Down 3 Up 1 Up 4 Down 5 Up

Bring the needle down to the back.

31

Make short and long stitches alternately, threading beads on the short stitches.

2 Down 4 Down 3 Up 5 Up 1 Up

Bring the needle down to the back.

32

3mm-long bugle bead 6mm-long bugle bead 4 Down 2 Down 1 Up 3 Up 5 Up

Thread 3mm-long and 6mm-long bugle beads alternately.

Bring the needle down to the back.

33

2 Down 4 Down 1 Up 3 Up 5 Up 4 3 2 Down 1 Up

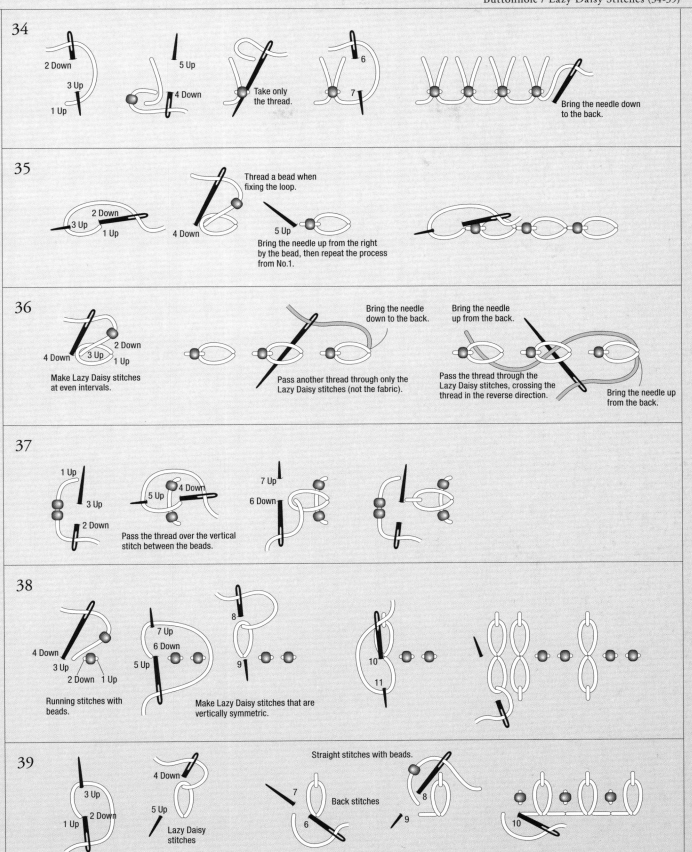

34

2 Down
3 Up
1 Up
5 Up
4 Down
Take only the thread.
6
7
Bring the needle down to the back.

35

2 Down
3 Up
1 Up
4 Down
Thread a bead when fixing the loop.
5 Up
Bring the needle up from the right by the bead, then repeat the process from No.1.

36

4 Down
3 Up
2 Down
1 Up
Make Lazy Daisy stitches at even intervals.
Bring the needle down to the back.
Pass another thread through only the Lazy Daisy stitches (not the fabric).
Bring the needle up from the back.
Pass the thread through the Lazy Daisy stitches, crossing the thread in the reverse direction.
Bring the needle up from the back.

37

1 Up
3 Up
2 Down
5 Up
4 Down
Pass the thread over the vertical stitch between the beads.
7 Up
6 Down

38

4 Down
3 Up
2 Down
1 Up
Running stitches with beads.
7 Up
6 Down
5 Up
8
9
Make Lazy Daisy stitches that are vertically symmetric.
10
11

39

3 Up
2 Down
1 Up
4 Down
5 Up
Lazy Daisy stitches
7
6
Back stitches
Straight stitches with beads.
8
9
10

69

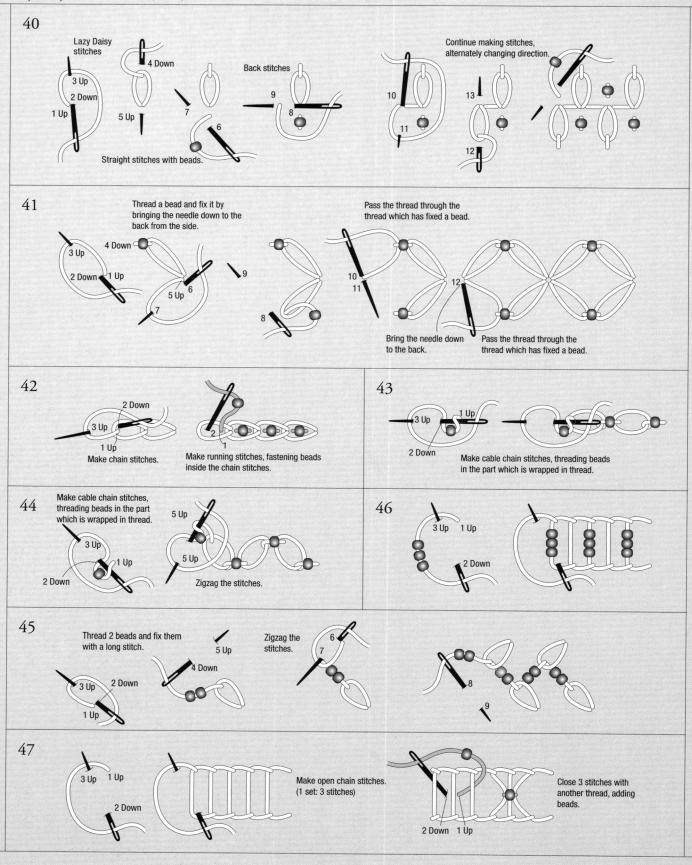

40

Lazy Daisy stitches

3 Up
2 Down
1 Up
4 Down
5 Up

Straight stitches with beads.

7
6

Back stitches

9
8

Continue making stitches, alternately changing direction.

10
11
12
13

41

Thread a bead and fix it by bringing the needle down to the back from the side.

3 Up
2 Down
1 Up
4 Down
5 Up
6
7
8
9

Pass the thread through the thread which has fixed a bead.

10
11
12

Bring the needle down to the back.

Pass the thread through the thread which has fixed a bead.

42

2 Down
3 Up
1 Up

Make chain stitches.

2
1

Make running stitches, fastening beads inside the chain stitches.

43

1 Up
3 Up
2 Down

Make cable chain stitches, threading beads in the part which is wrapped in thread.

44

Make cable chain stitches, threading beads in the part which is wrapped in thread.

3 Up
1 Up
2 Down
5 Up
5 Up

Zigzag the stitches.

46

3 Up
1 Up
2 Down

45

Thread 2 beads and fix them with a long stitch.

3 Up
2 Down
1 Up
5 Up
4 Down

Zigzag the stitches.

6
7
8
9

47

3 Up
1 Up
2 Down

Make open chain stitches. (1 set: 3 stitches)

Close 3 stitches with another thread, adding beads.

2 Down   1 Up

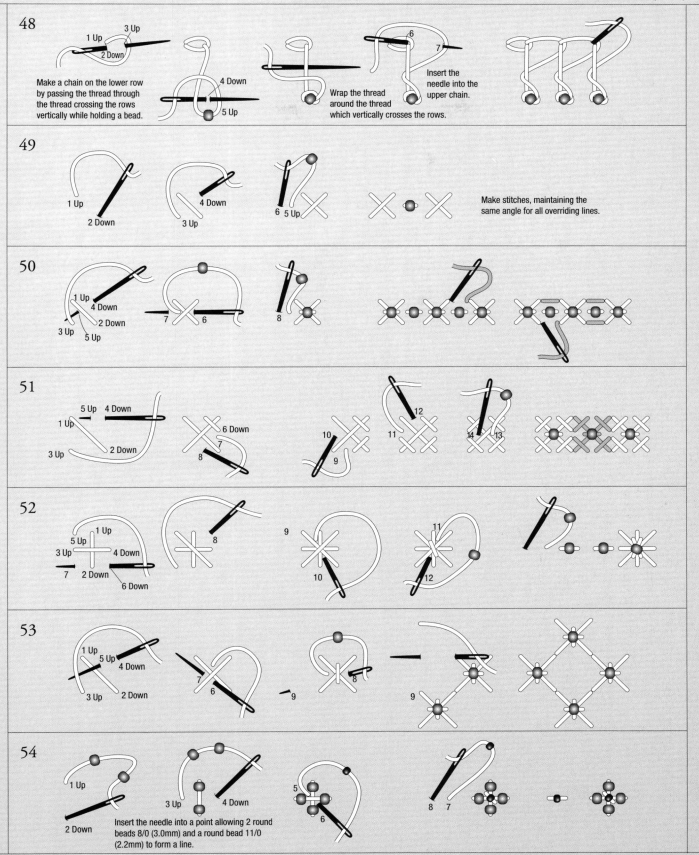

48

Make a chain on the lower row by passing the thread through the thread crossing the rows vertically while holding a bead.

1 Up
3 Up
2 Down
4 Down
5 Up

Wrap the thread around the thread which vertically crosses the rows.

6
7
Insert the needle into the upper chain.

49

1 Up
2 Down
4 Down
3 Up
6 5 Up

Make stitches, maintaining the same angle for all overriding lines.

50

1 Up
4 Down
2 Down
3 Up
5 Up
7 6
8

51

5 Up 4 Down
1 Up
3 Up 2 Down
6 Down
7
8
10
9
12
11
14 13

52

1 Up
5 Up
3 Up 4 Down
7 2 Down
6 Down
8
9
10
11
12

53

1 Up 5 Up
4 Down
3 Up 2 Down
7
6
8
9
9

54

1 Up
2 Down
3 Up
4 Down

Insert the needle into a point allowing 2 round beads 8/0 (3.0mm) and a round bead 11/0 (2.2mm) to form a line.

5
6
8 7

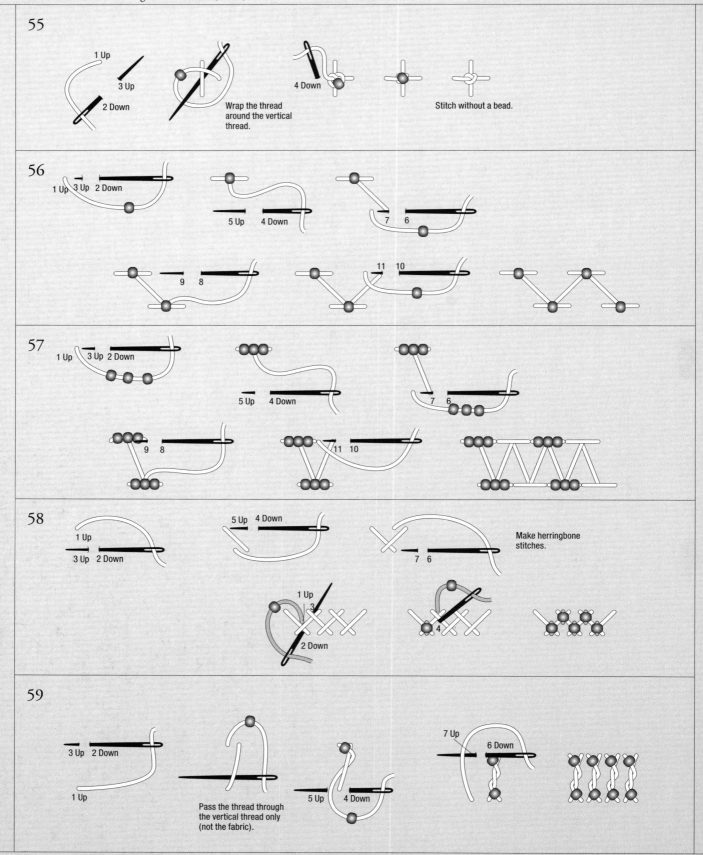

55

1 Up 3 Up 2 Down 4 Down

Wrap the thread around the vertical thread.

Stitch without a bead.

56

1 Up 3 Up 2 Down 5 Up 4 Down 7 6

9 8 11 10

57

1 Up 3 Up 2 Down 5 Up 4 Down 7 6

9 8 11 10

58

1 Up 3 Up 2 Down 5 Up 4 Down 7 6

Make herringbone stitches.

1 Up 3 2 Down 4

59

3 Up 2 Down 1 Up 7 Up 6 Down 5 Up 4 Down

Pass the thread through the vertical thread only (not the fabric).

60

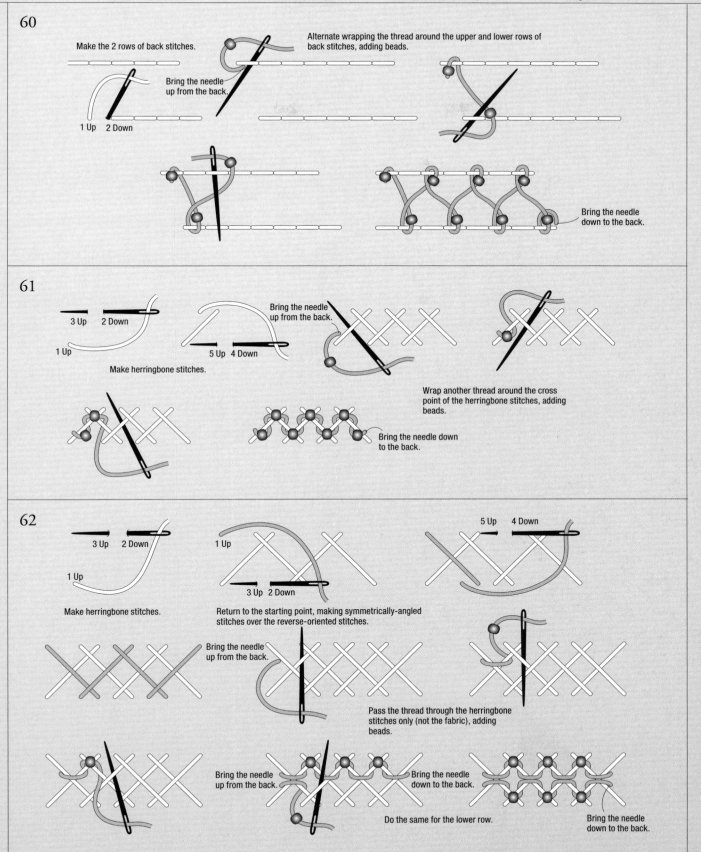

Make the 2 rows of back stitches.

Bring the needle up from the back.

Alternate wrapping the thread around the upper and lower rows of back stitches, adding beads.

1 Up   2 Down

Bring the needle down to the back.

61

3 Up   2 Down

1 Up

Make herringbone stitches.

Bring the needle up from the back.

5 Up   4 Down

Wrap another thread around the cross point of the herringbone stitches, adding beads.

Bring the needle down to the back.

62

3 Up   2 Down

1 Up

Make herringbone stitches.

1 Up

3 Up 2 Down

Return to the starting point, making symmetrically-angled stitches over the reverse-oriented stitches.

5 Up   4 Down

Bring the needle up from the back.

Pass the thread through the herringbone stitches only (not the fabric), adding beads.

Bring the needle up from the back.

Bring the needle down to the back.

Do the same for the lower row.

Bring the needle down to the back.

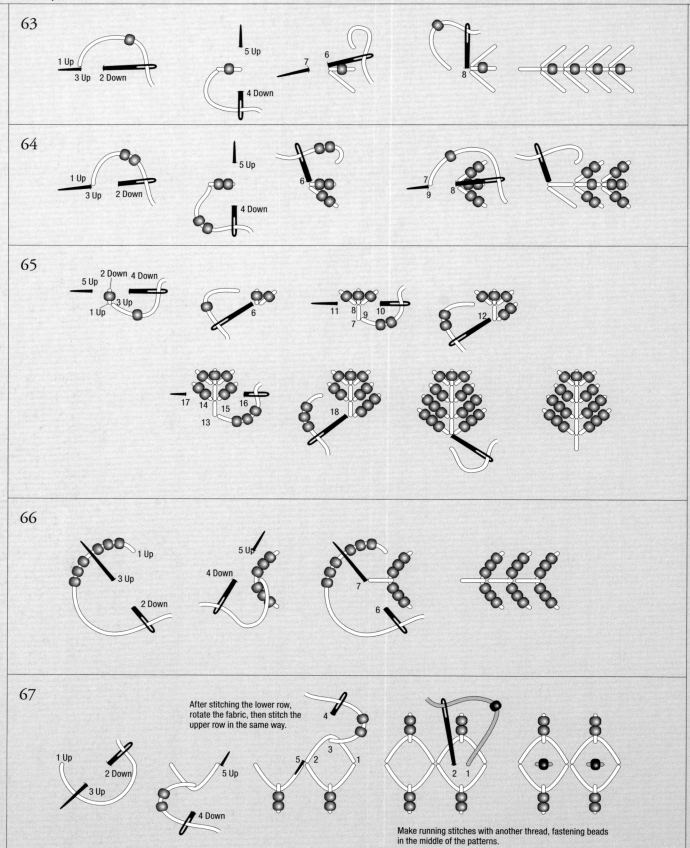

63

1 Up
3 Up 2 Down

5 Up
4 Down

7 6

8

64

1 Up
3 Up 2 Down

5 Up
4 Down

6

7
9 8

65

5 Up 2 Down 4 Down
1 Up 3 Up

6

11 8 10
7 9

12

17 14 15 16
13

18

66

1 Up
3 Up
2 Down

5 Up
4 Down

7
6

67

After stitching the lower row,
rotate the fabric, then stitch the
upper row in the same way.

4

1 Up
2 Down
3 Up

5 Up
4 Down

3
5 2 1

2 1

Make running stitches with another thread, fastening beads
in the middle of the patterns.

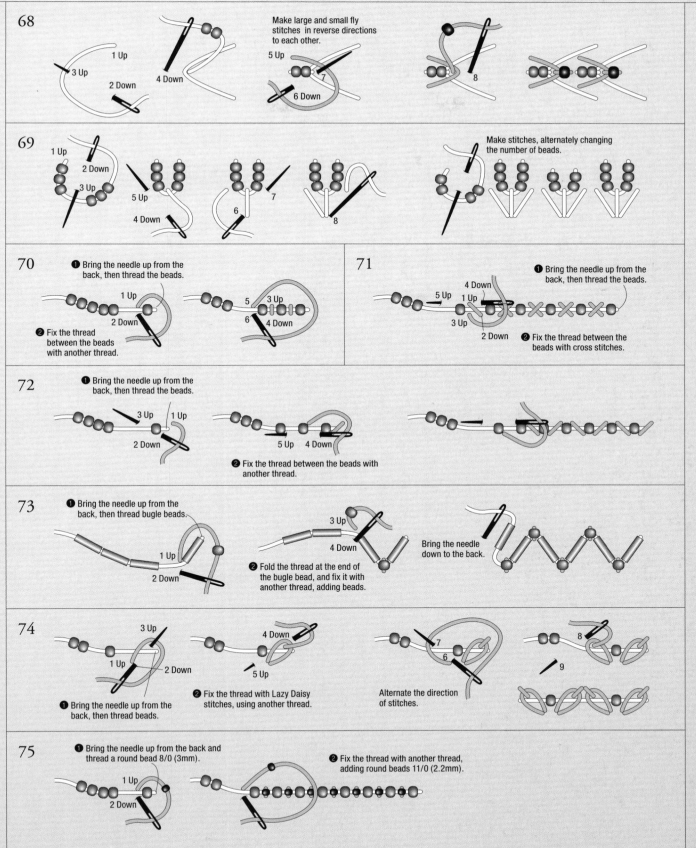

68

1 Up
3 Up
2 Down
4 Down

Make large and small fly stitches in reverse directions to each other.

5 Up
7
6 Down

8

69

1 Up
2 Down
3 Up
5 Up
4 Down
6
7
8

Make stitches, alternately changing the number of beads.

70

❶ Bring the needle up from the back, then thread the beads.

1 Up
2 Down

❷ Fix the thread between the beads with another thread.

5
6
3 Up
4 Down

71

❶ Bring the needle up from the back, then thread the beads.

4 Down
5 Up
1 Up
3 Up
2 Down

❷ Fix the thread between the beads with cross stitches.

72

❶ Bring the needle up from the back, then thread the beads.

3 Up
1 Up
2 Down

5 Up
4 Down

❷ Fix the thread between the beads with another thread.

73

❶ Bring the needle up from the back, then thread bugle beads.

1 Up
2 Down

3 Up
4 Down

❷ Fold the thread at the end of the bugle bead, and fix it with another thread, adding beads.

Bring the needle down to the back.

74

3 Up
1 Up
2 Down

4 Down
5 Up

❷ Fix the thread with Lazy Daisy stitches, using another thread.

7
6

Alternate the direction of stitches.

8
9

❶ Bring the needle up from the back, then thread beads.

75

❶ Bring the needle up from the back and thread a round bead 8/0 (3mm).

1 Up
2 Down

❷ Fix the thread with another thread, adding round beads 11/0 (2.2mm).

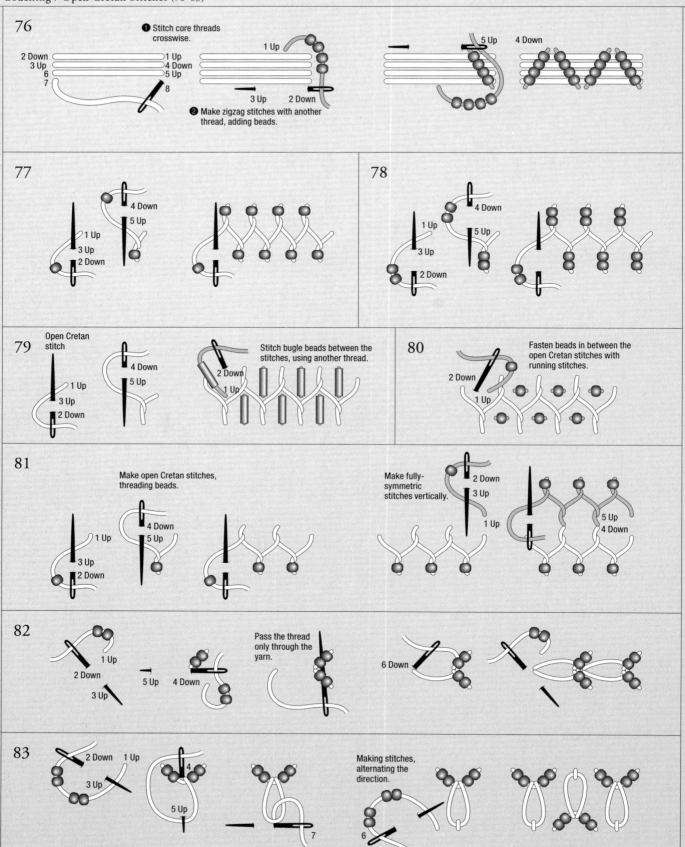

76

❶ Stitch core threads crosswise.

2 Down — 1 Up
3 Up — 4 Down
6 — 5 Up
7 — 8

1 Up
3 Up   2 Down
5 Up   4 Down

❷ Make zigzag stitches with another thread, adding beads.

77

1 Up
3 Up
2 Down
4 Down
5 Up

78

1 Up
3 Up
2 Down
4 Down
5 Up

79 Open Cretan stitch

1 Up
3 Up
2 Down
4 Down
5 Up

Stitch bugle beads between the stitches, using another thread.

2 Down
1 Up

80

Fasten beads in between the open Cretan stitches with running stitches.

2 Down
1 Up

81

Make open Cretan stitches, threading beads.

1 Up
3 Up
2 Down
4 Down
5 Up

Make fully-symmetric stitches vertically.

2 Down
3 Up
1 Up
5 Up
4 Down

82

1 Up
2 Down
3 Up
5 Up   4 Down

Pass the thread only through the yarn.

6 Down

83

2 Down   1 Up
3 Up
4
5 Up
7

Making stitches, alternating the direction.

6

76

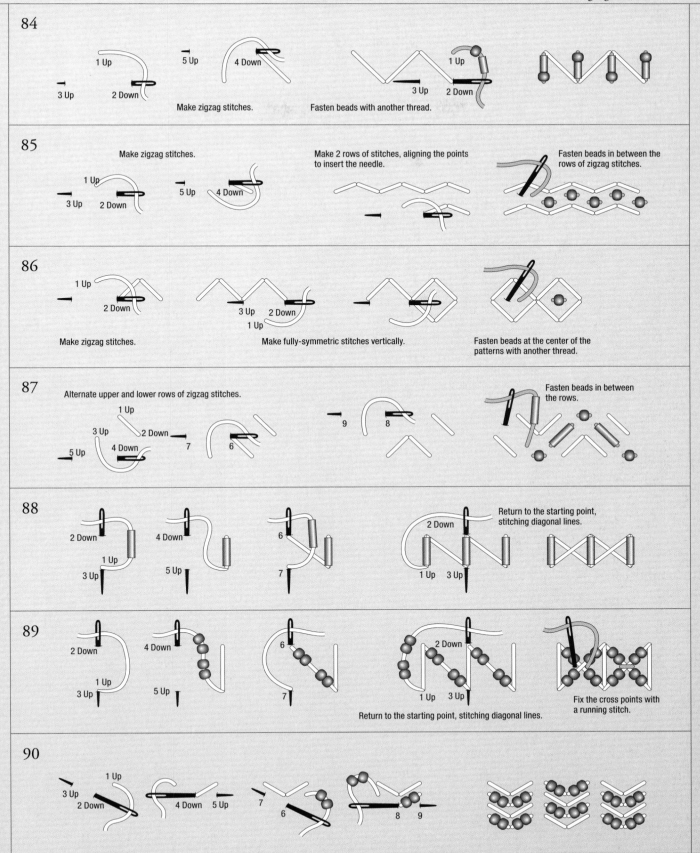

84

1 Up 5 Up 4 Down

3 Up 2 Down

Make zigzag stitches.

Fasten beads with another thread.

1 Up 3 Up 2 Down

85

Make zigzag stitches.

Make 2 rows of stitches, aligning the points to insert the needle.

Fasten beads in between the rows of zigzag stitches.

1 Up 5 Up 4 Down

3 Up 2 Down

86

1 Up

2 Down

3 Up 2 Down

1 Up

Make zigzag stitches.

Make fully-symmetric stitches vertically.

Fasten beads at the center of the patterns with another thread.

87

Alternate upper and lower rows of zigzag stitches.

1 Up

3 Up 2 Down

5 Up 4 Down 7 6 9 8

Fasten beads in between the rows.

88

2 Down 4 Down 6

1 Up 5 Up 7

3 Up

2 Down

1 Up 3 Up

Return to the starting point, stitching diagonal lines.

89

2 Down 4 Down 6

1 Up 5 Up 7

3 Up

Return to the starting point, stitching diagonal lines.

2 Down

1 Up 3 Up

Fix the cross points with a running stitch.

90

1 Up

3 Up

2 Down 4 Down 5 Up

7

6 8 9

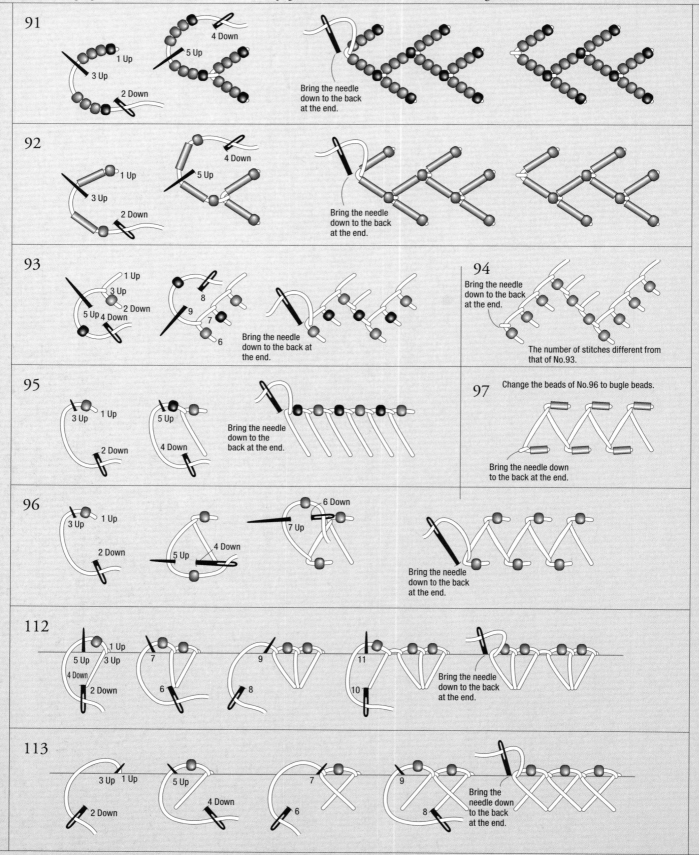

91

4 Down
1 Up
3 Up
5 Up
2 Down
Bring the needle down to the back at the end.

92

4 Down
1 Up
5 Up
3 Up
2 Down
Bring the needle down to the back at the end.

93

1 Up
3 Up
2 Down
5 Up 4 Down
8
9
7
6
Bring the needle down to the back at the end.

94

Bring the needle down to the back at the end.
The number of stitches different from that of No.93.

95

3 Up 1 Up
2 Down
5 Up
4 Down
Bring the needle down to the back at the end.

97

Change the beads of No.96 to bugle beads.
Bring the needle down to the back at the end.

96

3 Up 1 Up
2 Down
5 Up 4 Down
6 Down
7 Up
Bring the needle down to the back at the end.

112

1 Up
5 Up 3 Up
4 Down
2 Down
7
6
9
8
11
10
Bring the needle down to the back at the end.

113

3 Up 1 Up
2 Down
5 Up
4 Down
6
7
9
8
Bring the needle down to the back at the end.

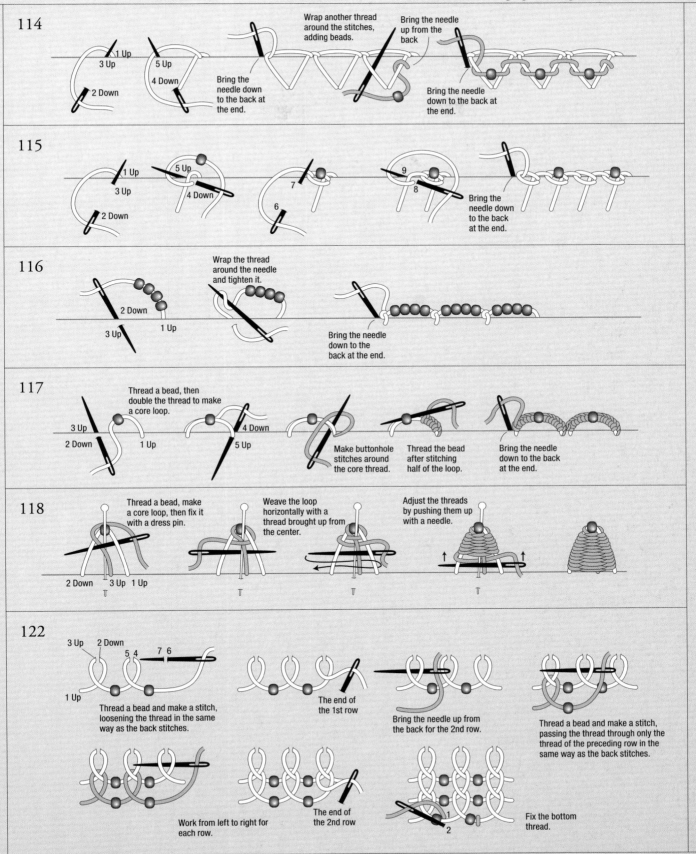

114

1 Up
3 Up
2 Down
5 Up
4 Down

Bring the needle down to the back at the end.

Wrap another thread around the stitches, adding beads.

Bring the needle up from the back

Bring the needle down to the back at the end.

115

1 Up
3 Up
2 Down
5 Up
4 Down
7
6
9
8

Bring the needle down to the back at the end.

116

2 Down
3 Up
1 Up

Wrap the thread around the needle and tighten it.

Bring the needle down to the back at the end.

117

3 Up
2 Down
1 Up

Thread a bead, then double the thread to make a core loop.

4 Down
5 Up

Make buttonhole stitches around the core thread.

Thread the bead after stitching half of the loop.

Bring the needle down to the back at the end.

118

Thread a bead, make a core loop, then fix it with a dress pin.

2 Down   3 Up   1 Up

Weave the loop horizontally with a thread brought up from the center.

Adjust the threads by pushing them up with a needle.

122

3 Up   2 Down
5 4   7 6
1 Up

Thread a bead and make a stitch, loosening the thread in the same way as the back stitches.

The end of the 1st row

Bring the needle up from the back for the 2nd row.

Thread a bead and make a stitch, passing the thread through only the thread of the preceding row in the same way as the back stitches.

Work from left to right for each row.

The end of the 2nd row

2
1

Fix the bottom thread.

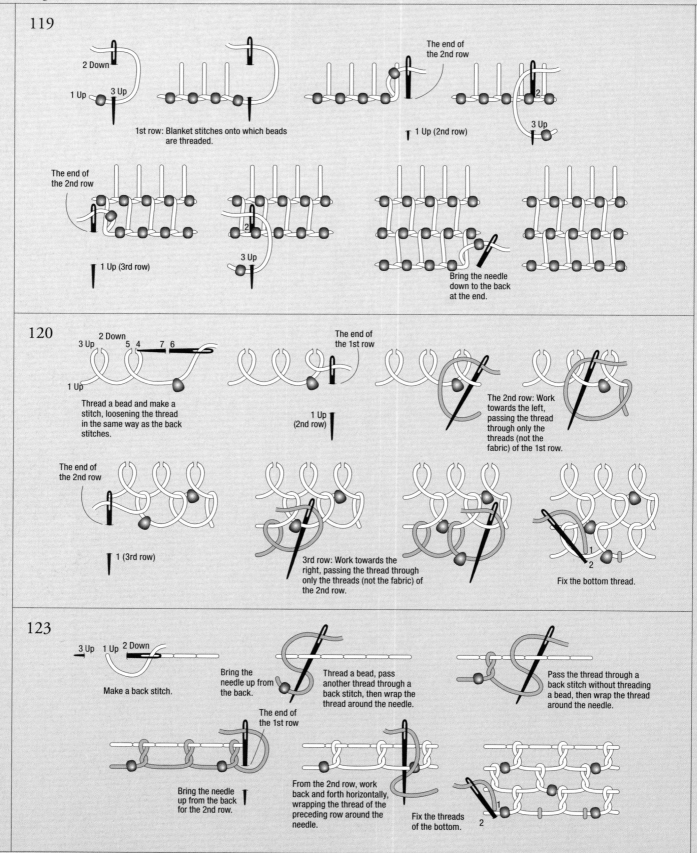

119

2 Down

1 Up 3 Up

1st row: Blanket stitches onto which beads are threaded.

The end of the 2nd row

1 Up (2nd row)

3 Up

The end of the 2nd row

1 Up (3rd row)

3 Up

Bring the needle down to the back at the end.

120

3 Up 2 Down

5 4 7 6

1 Up

Thread a bead and make a stitch, loosening the thread in the same way as the back stitches.

The end of the 1st row

1 Up (2nd row)

The 2nd row: Work towards the left, passing the thread through only the threads (not the fabric) of the 1st row.

The end of the 2nd row

1 (3rd row)

3rd row: Work towards the right, passing the thread through only the threads (not the fabric) of the 2nd row.

Fix the bottom thread.

1
2

123

3 Up 1 Up 2 Down

Make a back stitch.

Bring the needle up from the back.

Thread a bead, pass another thread through a back stitch, then wrap the thread around the needle.

Pass the thread through a back stitch without threading a bead, then wrap the thread around the needle.

The end of the 1st row

Bring the needle up from the back for the 2nd row.

From the 2nd row, work back and forth horizontally, wrapping the thread of the preceding row around the needle.

Fix the threads of the bottom.

1
2

80

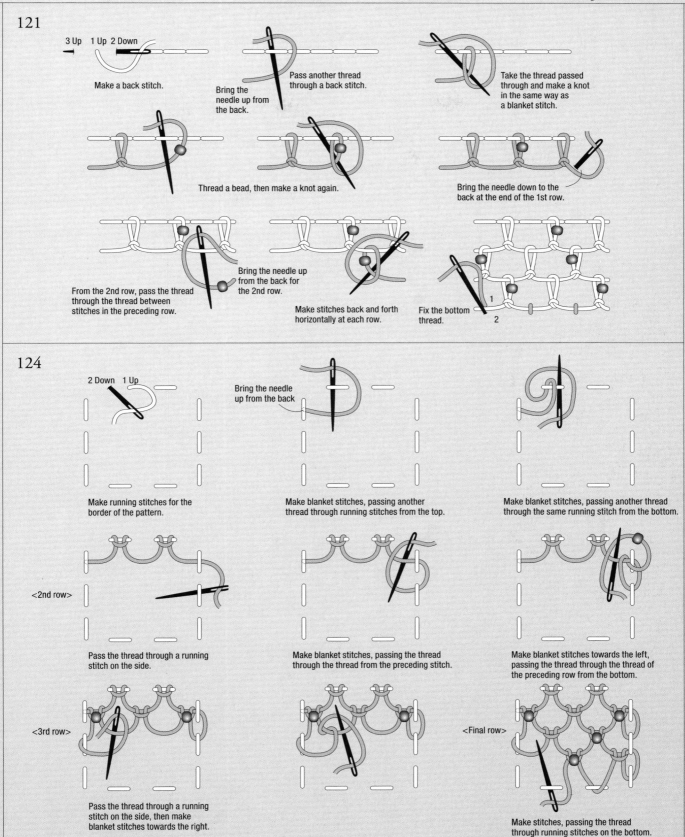

121

3 Up   1 Up   2 Down

Make a back stitch.

Bring the needle up from the back.

Pass another thread through a back stitch.

Take the thread passed through and make a knot in the same way as a blanket stitch.

Thread a bead, then make a knot again.

Bring the needle down to the back at the end of the 1st row.

From the 2nd row, pass the thread through the thread between stitches in the preceding row.

Bring the needle up from the back for the 2nd row.

Make stitches back and forth horizontally at each row.

Fix the bottom thread.

1
2

124

2 Down   1 Up

Make running stitches for the border of the pattern.

Bring the needle up from the back

Make blanket stitches, passing another thread through running stitches from the top.

Make blanket stitches, passing another thread through the same running stitch from the bottom.

<2nd row>

Pass the thread through a running stitch on the side.

Make blanket stitches, passing the thread through the thread from the preceding stitch.

Make blanket stitches towards the left, passing the thread through the thread of the preceding row from the bottom.

<3rd row>

Pass the thread through a running stitch on the side, then make blanket stitches towards the right.

<Final row>

Make stitches, passing the thread through running stitches on the bottom.

98

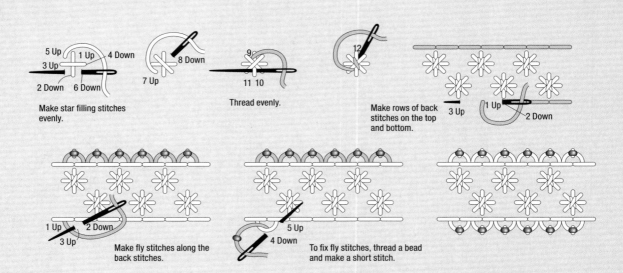

5 Up   1 Up   4 Down
3 Up
2 Down   6 Down

Make star filling stitches evenly.

8 Down
7 Up

9
11   10

Thread evenly.

12

Make rows of back stitches on the top and bottom.

3 Up
1 Up
2 Down

1 Up   2 Down
3 Up

Make fly stitches along the back stitches.

5 Up
4 Down

To fix fly stitches, thread a bead and make a short stitch.

99

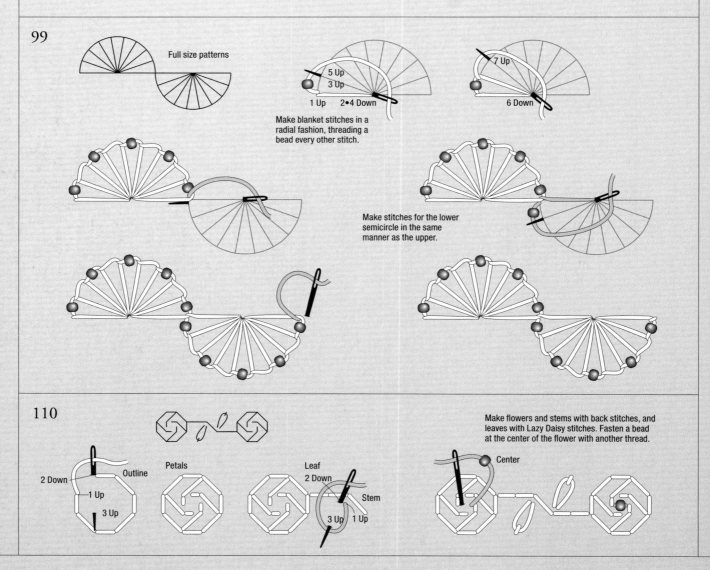

Full size patterns

5 Up
3 Up
1 Up   2•4 Down

Make blanket stitches in a radial fashion, threading a bead every other stitch.

7 Up
6 Down

Make stitches for the lower semicircle in the same manner as the upper.

110

Make flowers and stems with back stitches, and leaves with Lazy Daisy stitches. Fasten a bead at the center of the flower with another thread.

2 Down
1 Up
3 Up
Outline

Petals

Leaf
2 Down
3 Up   1 Up
Stem

Center

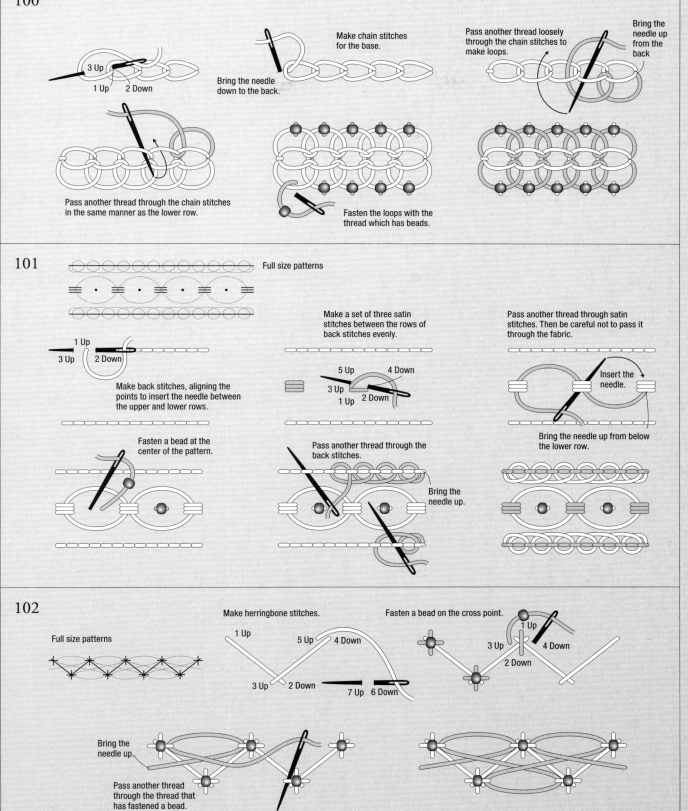

100

3 Up
1 Up   2 Down

Make chain stitches for the base.

Bring the needle down to the back.

Pass another thread loosely through the chain stitches to make loops.

Bring the needle up from the back

Pass another thread through the chain stitches in the same manner as the lower row.

Fasten the loops with the thread which has beads.

101

Full size patterns

1 Up
3 Up   2 Down

Make back stitches, aligning the points to insert the needle between the upper and lower rows.

Make a set of three satin stitches between the rows of back stitches evenly.

5 Up   4 Down
3 Up
1 Up   2 Down

Pass another thread through satin stitches. Then be careful not to pass it through the fabric.

Insert the needle.

Fasten a bead at the center of the pattern.

Pass another thread through the back stitches.

Bring the needle up.

Bring the needle up from below the lower row.

102

Full size patterns

Make herringbone stitches.

1 Up
5 Up   4 Down
3 Up   2 Down
7 Up   6 Down

Fasten a bead on the cross point.

1 Up
3 Up   4 Down
2 Down

Bring the needle up.

Pass another thread through the thread that has fastened a bead.

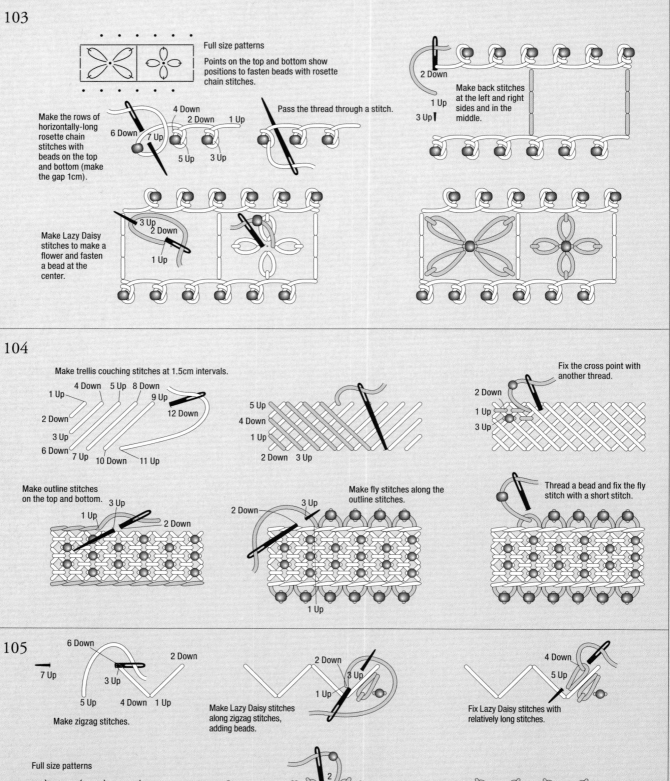

103

Full size patterns

Points on the top and bottom show positions to fasten beads with rosette chain stitches.

Make the rows of horizontally-long rosette chain stitches with beads on the top and bottom (make the gap 1cm).

4 Down
2 Down
1 Up
6 Down
7 Up
5 Up
3 Up

Pass the thread through a stitch.

2 Down
1 Up
3 Up

Make back stitches at the left and right sides and in the middle.

Make Lazy Daisy stitches to make a flower and fasten a bead at the center.

3 Up
2 Down
1 Up

104

Make trellis couching stitches at 1.5cm intervals.

1 Up
4 Down
5 Up
8 Down
9 Up
2 Down
12 Down
3 Up
6 Down
7 Up
10 Down
11 Up

5 Up
4 Down
1 Up
2 Down
3 Up

Fix the cross point with another thread.

2 Down
1 Up
3 Up

Make outline stitches on the top and bottom.

3 Up
1 Up
2 Down

Make fly stitches along the outline stitches.

2 Down
3 Up
1 Up

Thread a bead and fix the fly stitch with a short stitch.

105

6 Down
2 Down
7 Up
3 Up
5 Up
4 Down
1 Up

Make zigzag stitches.

2 Down
3 Up
1 Up

Make Lazy Daisy stitches along zigzag stitches, adding beads.

4 Down
5 Up

Fix Lazy Daisy stitches with relatively long stitches.

Full size patterns

2
1

106

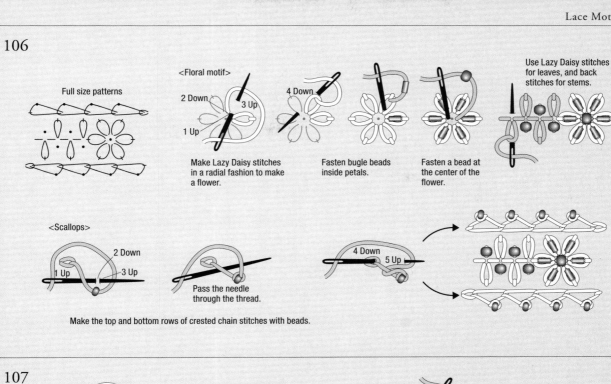

Full size patterns

<Floral motif>

2 Down
3 Up
1 Up

Make Lazy Daisy stitches in a radial fashion to make a flower.

4 Down

Fasten bugle beads inside petals.

Fasten a bead at the center of the flower.

Use Lazy Daisy stitches for leaves, and back stitches for stems.

<Scallops>

2 Down
1 Up
3 Up

Pass the needle through the thread.

4 Down
5 Up

Make the top and bottom rows of crested chain stitches with beads.

107

1 Up
3 Up 2 Down

5 Up 4 Down

Make Maltese stitches, being sure to make even loops.

Fasten the loop of Maltese stitch with a fly stitch onto which a bead is threaded.

Make back stitches to make a row parallel to the Maltese stitches.

Make running stitches, adding beads in between the rows.

Full size patterns

108

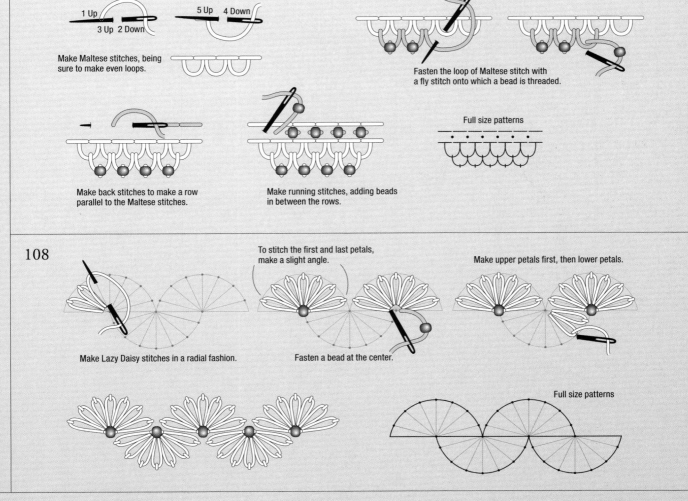

To stitch the first and last petals, make a slight angle.

Make upper petals first, then lower petals.

Make Lazy Daisy stitches in a radial fashion.

Fasten a bead at the center.

Full size patterns

109

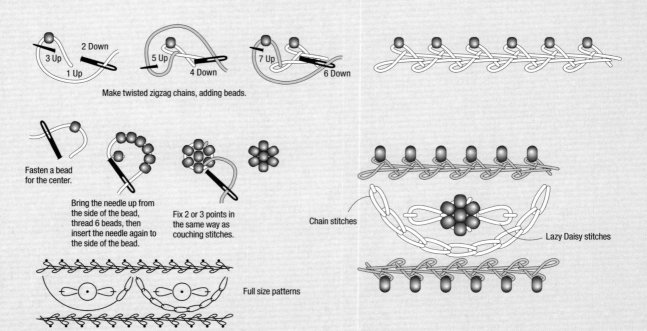

Make twisted zigzag chains, adding beads.

3 Up / 1 Up / 2 Down
5 Up / 4 Down
7 Up / 6 Down

Fasten a bead for the center.

Bring the needle up from the side of the bead, thread 6 beads, then insert the needle again to the side of the bead.

Fix 2 or 3 points in the same way as couching stitches.

Chain stitches

Lazy Daisy stitches

Full size patterns

111

Cross stitch chart

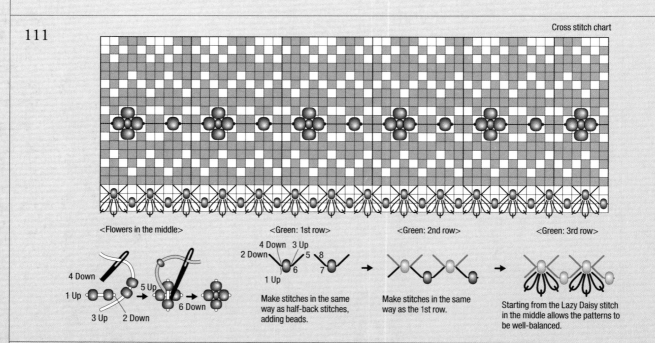

<Flowers in the middle>   <Green: 1st row>   <Green: 2nd row>   <Green: 3rd row>

4 Down
1 Up
3 Up   2 Down
5 Up
6 Down

4 Down 3 Up
2 Down   5   8
6
1 Up   7

Make stitches in the same way as half-back stitches, adding beads.

Make stitches in the same way as the 1st row.

Starting from the Lazy Daisy stitch in the middle allows the patterns to be well-balanced.

Tips   How to take care of your embroidery items...

After making an item with cute beaded embroidery, wouldn't you prefer to keep it pristine for as long as possible? Then take special care of it, handling the beads and base fabrics carefully.

• To clean the item, hand-wash gently after turning it inside-out so the beaded surface is inside. When using a washing machine, make sure the item is placed in a cleaning net.
• To dry the item, ensuring the beaded surface is on the inside and airing it in the shade will prevent discoloration of the beads.

• Washing is not recommended for some beads and spangles, so don't forget to check the instructions before using!

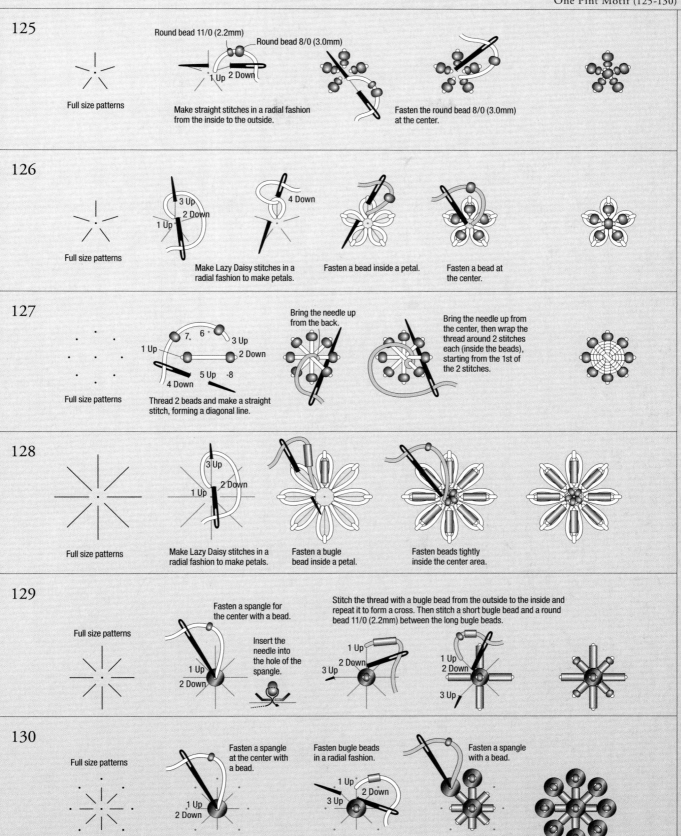

125

Full size patterns

Round bead 11/0 (2.2mm)

Round bead 8/0 (3.0mm)

1 Up   2 Down

Make straight stitches in a radial fashion from the inside to the outside.

Fasten the round bead 8/0 (3.0mm) at the center.

126

Full size patterns

3 Up

2 Down

1 Up

4 Down

Make Lazy Daisy stitches in a radial fashion to make petals.

Fasten a bead inside a petal.

Fasten a bead at the center.

127

Full size patterns

7. 6   3 Up

1 Up   2 Down

4 Down   5 Up   ·8

Thread 2 beads and make a straight stitch, forming a diagonal line.

Bring the needle up from the back.

Bring the needle up from the center, then wrap the thread around 2 stitches each (inside the beads), starting from the 1st of the 2 stitches.

128

Full size patterns

3 Up

2 Down

1 Up

Make Lazy Daisy stitches in a radial fashion to make petals.

Fasten a bugle bead inside a petal.

Fasten beads tightly inside the center area.

129

Full size patterns

Fasten a spangle for the center with a bead.

Insert the needle into the hole of the spangle.

1 Up

2 Down

Stitch the thread with a bugle bead from the outside to the inside and repeat it to form a cross. Then stitch a short bugle bead and a round bead 11/0 (2.2mm) between the long bugle beads.

1 Up

2 Down

3 Up

1 Up

2 Down

3 Up

130

Full size patterns

Fasten a spangle at the center with a bead.

1 Up

2 Down

Fasten bugle beads in a radial fashion.

1 Up

2 Down

3 Up

Fasten a spangle with a bead.

- The following list shows materials used for the samplers in order of threads (yarn count/color number/color/number of yarns) and beads (type/color number/color).
- The color numbers are from DMC for all embroidery threads and TOHO Beads for beads.

p.16 Running Stitches

1　No.5 3689 (pink) / round bead 8/0 (3.0mm) 919 (blue), 905 (pink), 901 (yellow) & 943 (pale purple)

2　No.5 3689 (pink) / round bead 8/0 (3.0mm) 919 (blue), 901 (yellow) & 173 (lime green)

3　No.5 ECRU (natural undyed color) / round bead 8/0 (3.0mm) 167 (green), 401 (white), 405 (red), 402 (yellow), 942 (dark blue), 403 (blue) & 174 (orange)

4　No.5 3689 (pink) / round bead 8/0 (3.0mm) 919 (blue), 905 (pink), 901 (yellow) & 943 (pale purple)

5　[Above] No.5 (aqua) / round bead 8/0 (3.0mm) (blue) [Below] No.5 3689 (pink) / round bead 8/0 (3.0mm) 905 (pink)

6　No.5 471 (green)/ round bead 8/0 (3.0mm) 173 (lime green)

p. 20 Straight Stitches

7　No.5 517 (blue) / round bead 8/0 (3.0mm) 405 (red)

8　No.5 905 (green) / round bead 8/0 (3.0mm) 174 (orange)

9　No.5 972 (yellow) / round bead 8/0 (3.0mm) 165 (red) & 167 (green)

10　No.5 321 (red) / round bead 8/0 (3.0mm) 22 (gold)

11　No.5 905 (green) / round bead 8/0 (3.0mm) 405 (red)

12　No.5 3350 (dark pink) / round bead 8/0 (3.0mm) 905 (pink)

13　No.25 721 (orange, quadruple yarn) / round bead 8/0 (3.0mm) 163 (blue), 165 (red), 167 (green) & 174 (orange)

p.22 Back/Pekinese Stitches

14　No.5 321 (red) / round bead 8/0 (3.0mm) 109 (red) / 174 (orange color) , 175 (yellow), 264 (turquoise blue) & 22 (gold)

15　No.5 321 (red) & 841 (beige) / round bead 8/0 (3.0mm) 175 (yellow), 174 (orange), 109 (red), 264 (turquoise blue) & 170 (pale blue)

16　No.5 321 (red) & 841 (beige) / round bead 8/0 (3.0mm) 22 (gold)

17　No.5 321 (red) & 841 (beige) / round bead 8/0 (3.0mm) 405 (red)

18　No.5 321 (red) & 841 (beige) / round bead 8/0 (3.0mm) 557 (gold)

19　No.5 321 (red) & 841 (beige) / round bead 8/0 (3.0mm) 173 (pale green), 175 (yellow), 174 (orange), 109 (red) & 264 (turquoise blue)

20　No.25 321 (red, triple yarn) / round bead 11/0 (2.2mm) 165 (red), 23 (aqua), 164 (lime green), 175 (yellow), 191c (pink), 174 (orange), 163 (blue), 101 (clear), 938 (dark blue) & 558 (platinum)

p.24 Outline/Holbein Stitches

21　No.5 841 (beige) / round bead 8/0 (3.0mm) 105 (lime green), 402 (yellow), 174 (orange), 125 (red) & 331 (dark red)

22　No.5 841 (beige) / round bead 8/0 (3.0mm) 174 (orange), 402 (yellow), 105 (lime green) & 125 (red)

23　No.5 841 (beige) / round bead 8/0 (3.0mm) 105 (lime green), 402 (yellow), 174 (orange), 125 (red) & 331 (dark red)

24　No.5 972 (yellow) / round bead 8/0 (3.0mm) 165 (red) & 167 (green)

25　No.5 905 (green) / round bead 8/0 (3.0mm) 174 (orange) & 405 (red)

26　No.5 841 (beige) / round bead 8/0 (3.0mm) 331 (dark red), 402 (yellow) & 174 (orange)

27　No.5 321 (red) / round bead 8/0 (3.0mm) 174 (orange) & 167 (green)

p.26 Blanket/Buttonhole Stitches

28　No.25 3013 (grass green, quadruple yarn) / round bead 8/0 (3.0mm) 557 (gold)

29　No.25 3013 (grass green, quadruple yarn) / round bead 8/0 (3.0mm) 173 (pale green), 105 (lime green) & 557 (gold)

30　No.25 3013 (grass green, quadruple yarn) / round bead 8/0 (3.0mm) 407 (green)

31　No.25 3023 (light ash green, quadruple yarn) / round bead 8/0 (3.0mm) 164 (lime green)

32　No.25 3013 (grass green, quadruple yarn) / round bead 11/0 (2.2mm) 402 (yellow), 3mm-long bugle bead 7 (green) & 6mm-long bugle bead 111 (dark yellow)

33　No.25 3032 (olive, quadruple yarn) / round bead 8/0 (3.0mm) 167 (green), 407 (green), 402 (yellow) & 557 (gold)

34　No.25 3032 (olive, quadruple yarn) / round bead 8/0 (3.0mm) 402 (yellow)

p.30 Lazy Daisy Stitches

35　No.25 899 (pink, quadruple yarn) / round bead 8/0 (3.0mm) 906 (pink)

36　No.5 3805 (dark pink, quadruple yarn), No.5 ECRU (natural undyed color)/ round bead 8/0 (3.0mm) 557 (gold)

37　No.25 3607 (purple pink, quadruple yarn) / round bead 11/0 (2.2mm) 558 (platinum)

38　No.25 3805 (dark pink, quadruple yarn) / round bead 11/0 (2.2mm) 332 (red-purple)

39　No.25 899 (pink, triple yarn) / round bead 11/0 (2.2mm) 557 (gold)

40　No.25 3607 (purple pink, triple yarn) / round bead 11/0 (2.2mm) 264 (turquoise blue)

41　No.25 3805 (dark pink, triple yarn) / round bead 8/0 (3.0mm) 558 (platinum)

p.32 Chain Stitches

42　No.25 326 (dark pink, quadruple yarn) / round bead 8/0 (3.0mm) 558 (gold)

43　No.25 550 (dark purple, quadruple yarn) / round bead 8/0 (3.0mm) 264 191c (pink)

44　No.25 208 (purple, triple yarn) / round bead 8/0 (3.0mm) 264 (turquoise blue)

45　No.25 917 (pink, triple yarn) / round bead 11/0 (2.2mm) 558 (platinum)

46　No.25 554 (pale purple, quadruple yarn) / round bead 11/0 (2.2mm) 170 (pale blue), 105 (lime green), 104 (turquoise), 252 (purple) & 558 (platinum)

47　No.25 554 (pale purple, quadruple yarn) / round bead 8/0 (3.0mm) 943 (light purple), 977 (pale purple) & 252 (purple)

48　No.25 209 (light purple, quadruple yarn) / round bead 8/0 (3.0mm) 559 (gold), 252 (purple) & 977 (light purple)

p.34 Cross Stitches

49　No.25 3765 (blue, triple yarn) / round bead 11/0 (2.2mm) 405 (red)

50　No.25 3765 (blue, triple yarn)& 3865 (white, triple yarn) / round bead 11/0 (2.2mm) 22 (gold) & 332 (red-purple)

51　No.25 3765 (blue, quadruple yarn)& 3865 (white, quadruple yarn) / round bead 8/0 (3.0mm) 558 (platinum)

52　No.25 3765 (blue, quadruple yarn) / round bead 8/0 (3.0mm) 557 (gold)

53　No.25 3765 (blue, triple yarn) / round bead 11/0 (2.2mm) 165 (red)

54　No.25 3865 (white, triple yarn)/ round bead 8/0 (3.0mm) 332 (red-purple) & round bead 11/0 (2.2mm) 559 (gold)

55　No.25 3765 (blue, quadruple yarn) / round bead 8/0 (3.0mm) 558 (platinum)

p.36 Chevron/Herringbone Stitches

56　No.25 BLANC (white, quadruple yarn) / round bead 8/0 (3.0mm) 148 (cream)

57　No.5 ECRU (natural undyed color) / round bead 11/0 (2.2mm) 401 (white) & round bead 8/0 (3.0mm) 148 (cream)

58　No.25 738 (beige, quadruple yarn) & BLANC (white, quadruple yarn) / round bead 8/0 (3.0mm) 401 (white)

59　No.25 BLANC (white, quadruple yarn) / round bead 8/0 (3.0mm) 148 (cream)

60　No.25 738 (beige, quadruple yarn) & ECRU (natural undyed color, quadruple yarn) / round bead 8/0 (3.0mm) 401 (white)

61　No.25 BLANC (white, quadruple yarn) / E3821 (gold, triple yarn) / round bead 8/0 (3.0mm) 401 (white), 148 (cream) & 557 (gold)

62　No.25 BLANC (white, quadruple yarn), 738 (beige, quadruple yarn)& E3821 (gold, triple yarn) / round bead 8/0 (3.0mm) 401 (white), 148 (cream) & 557 (gold)

p. 38 Fern/Fly Stitches

63　No.25 3346 (green, quadruple yarn) / round bead 8/0 (3.0mm) 174 (orange), 165 (red)

64　No.25 3346 (green, quadruple yarn) / round bead 11/0 (2.2mm) 402 (yellow), 332 (red purple)

65　No.25 433 (brown, quadruple yarn) / round bead 11/0 (2.2mm) 167 (green), 30 (orange), round bead 8/0 (3.0mm) 405 (red)

66　No.25 973 (yellow, quadruple yarn) / round bead 11/0 (2.2mm) 167 (green), 24 (lime green), 175 (yellow)

67　No.25 3347 (grass green, quadruple yarn) / round bead 11/0 (2.2mm) 174 (orange), 175 (yellow) /round bead 8/0 (3.0mm) 264 (turquoise blue)

68　No.25 3347 (grass green, quadruple yarn) / round bead 8/0 (3.0mm) 174 (orange), 175 (yellow)

69　No.25 987 (green, quadruple yarn) / round bead 8/0 (3.0mm) 401 (white) & 402 (yellow)

p. 40 Couting Stitches

70　No.25 353 (coral pink, quadruple yarn), 739 (cream, quadruple yarn) / round bead 8/0 (3.0mm) 905 (pink)

71　No.25 353 (coral pink, quadruple yarn), 739 (cream, quadruple yarn)/ 122 (milk)

72　No.25 353 (coral pink, quadruple yarn) 819 (pale pink, quadruple yarn) / round bead 8/0 (3.0mm) 122 (milk), 169 (pale pink) & 905 (pink)

73　No.25 353 (coral pink, quadruple yarn) 819 (pale pink, quadruple yarn)/6mm-long bugle bead 122 (milk), round bead 8/0 (3.0mm) 905 (pink)

74　No.25 819 (pale pink, quadruple yarn), 353 (coral pink, quadruple yarn)/round bead 8/0 (3.0mm) 905 (pink), 169 (pale pink) & 557 (gold)

75　No.25 353 (coral pink, quadruple yarn), 739 (cream, double yarn) / round bead 8/0 (3.0mm) 905 (pink), 2 mm pearl 200 (white)

76　No.25 739 (cream, quadruple yarn), 353 (coral pink, double yarn)/round bead 11/0 (2.2mm) 122 (milk), 904 (light orange) & 558 (Platinum)

p.42 Open Cretan Stitches

77　No.25 738 (beige, quadruple yarn)/round bead 8/0 (3.0mm) 122 (milk), 903 (cream) & 558 (platinum)

78　No.25 3864 (pink beige, quadruple yarn)/ round bead 8/0 (3.0mm) 122 (milk), 164 (lime green)

79　No.25 738 (beige, quadruple yarn), sewing yarn #60 (white)/6mm-long bugle bead 329 (brown), 122 (milk) & 44 (lime green)

80　No.25 3864 (dark beige, quadruple yarn), 738 (beige, double yarn) / round bead 8/0 (3.0mm) 903 (cream), 122 (milk) & 164 (lime green)

81　No.25 3864 (pink beige, quadruple yarn)/round bead 8/0 (3.0mm) 557 (platinum), 122 (milk) & 162 (light brown)

82　No.25 3864 (pink beige, quadruple yarn)/122 (milk), -903 (cream) & 164 (lime green)

83   No.25 3863 (dark beige)/round bead 8/0 (3.0mm) 558 (platinum), 122 (milk) & 903 (cream)

p.44 **Zigzag Stitches**

84   No.25 747 (aqua, quadruple yarn; double yarn when threading beads)/ 3mm-long bugle bead 168 (blue), round bead 11/0 (2.2mm) 104 (aqua)

85   No.25 3811 (light saxe blue, quadruple yarn)/ round bead 11/0 (2.2mm) 104 (aqua), 107 (blue) & 170 (pale blue)

86   No.25 598 (saxe blue, quadruple yarn)/round bead 8/0 (3.0mm) 173 (pale green)

87   No.25 598 (saxe blue, quadruple yarn)/6mm-long bugle bead 3 (aqua), round bead 8/0 (3.0mm) 920 (saxe blue)

88   No.25 597 (dark saxe blue, quadruple yarn)/6mm-long bugle bead 3 (aqua), 23 (aqua) & 21 (silver)

89   No.25 597 (dark saxe blue, quadruple yarn)/ round bead 11/0 (2.2mm) 104 (aqua) & 105 (lime green)

90   No.25 3810 (blue, quadruple yarn)/ round bead 11/0 (2.2mm) 403 (aqua) & 163 (blue)

p.46 **Feather Stitches**

91   No.25 518 (blue, double yarn)/ round bead 11/0 (2.2mm) 931 (blue), 558 (platinum)

92   No.25 498 (red, double yarn)/3mm-long bugle bead 45 (red), round bead 11/0 (2.2mm) 558 (platinum)

93   No.25 898 (brown, quadruple yarn)/round bead 8/0 (3.0mm) 332 (red-purple), 558 (platinum) & 559 (gold)

94   No.25 498 (red, quadruple yarn) / round bead 8/0 (3.0mm) 264 (turquoise blue)

95   No.25 600 (dark pink) / round bead 8/0 (3.0mm) 559 (gold) & 329 (brown)

96   No.25 898 (brown, quadruple yarn)/round bead 8/0 (3.0mm) 23 (aqua)

97   No.25 498 (red, quadruple yarn) / 3mm-long bugle bead 22 (gold)

p.48 **Lace Stitches**

98, 99, 107 &109   No.12 B5200 (white)/round bead 11/0 (2.2mm) 401 (white)

100   No.8 ECRU (natural undyed color), B5200 (white), sewing yarn #60 (white)/ round bead 11/0 (2.2mm) 401 (white)

101   No.12 B5200 (white)/ No.8 ECRU (natural undyed color), B5200 (white)/ 2 mm pearl 200 (white)

102   No.12 ECRU (natural undyed color), B5200 (white) /round bead 8/0 (3.0mm) 401 (white)

103   No.12 B5200 (white)/round bead 11/0 (2.2mm), round bead 8/0 (3.0mm) 401 (white)

104   No.12 B5200 (white)/round bead 11/0 (2.2mm) 21 (Silver), 2 mm pearl 200 (white)

105   No.12 B5200 (white)/ 2 mm Pearl 200 (white)

106   No. 12 & 8 B5200 (white) /round bead 11/0 (2.2mm), 3mm-long bugle bead, round bead 8/0 (3.0mm) 401 (white)

108   No.12 B5200 (white)/round bead 8/0 (3.0mm) 401 (white)

110   No.8 B5200 (white)/round bead 11/0 (2.2mm) 401 (white)

111   No.12 B5200 (white)/round bead 11/0 (2.2mm), round bead 8/0 (3.0mm) 401 (white), round bead 11/0 (2.2mm) 21 (silver)

p.54 **Edging Stitches**

112   No.25 3804 (dark pink, quadruple yarn) / round bead 8/0 (3.0mm) 404 (lime green)

113   No.25 498 (red, quadruple yarn) /round bead 8/0 (3.0mm) 165 (red), 174 (orange) & 557 (gold)

114   No.25 898 (brown, quadruple yarn)/741 (orange, quadruple yarn)/round bead 8/0 (3.0mm) 563 (metallic pink)

115   No.25 603 (pink, triple yarn)/round bead 8/0 (3.0mm) 329 (brown)

116   No.25 721 (orange, triple yarn)/round bead 11/0 (2.2mm) 909 (pink), 405 (red), 174 (orange) & 329 (brown)

117   No.25 498 (red), 603 (pink) & 721 (orange); Quadruple yarn for all the beads. / round bead 8/0 (3.0mm) 557 (gold)

118   No.25 3804 (dark pink), 721 (orange); Quadruple yarn for all the beads. /round bead 8/0 (3.0mm) 557 (gold) & 563 (metallic pink)

p.56 **Filling Stitches**

• The threads are hemp yarn (ramie), and medium-thin (yarn count 4) sewing thread (natural)

119   [Left] round bead 8/0 (3.0mm) 174 (orange), 165 (red)/ [Middle] round bead 8/0 (3.0mm) 163 (aqua) & 401 (white)/ [Right] round bead 8/0 (3.0mm) 175 (yellow) & 164 (lime green)

120   [Left] Magatama bead 4mm M25 (red)/[Middle] Magatama bead 5mm M248 (blue)/[Right] Magatama bead 4mm M43 (aqua)

121   [Left] round bead 8/0 (3.0mm) 23 (aqua)/[Middle] round bead 8/0 (3.0mm) 402 (yellow)/[Right]round bead 8/0 (3.0mm) 27 (green)

122   [Left] round bead 8/0 (3.0mm) 264 (turquoise blue)/ [Middle] round bead 8/0 (3.0mm) 174 (orange)/[Right] round bead 8/0 (3.0mm) 104 (aqua)

123   [Left] round bead 8/0 (3.0mm) 405 (red)/[Middle] round bead 8/0 (3.0mm) 403 (aqua)/ [Right] round bead 8/0 (3.0mm) 404 (lime green)

124   [Left] round bead 8/0 (3.0mm) 175 (yellow)/[Middle] round bead 8/0 (3.0mm) 165 (red)/[Right] round bead 8/0 (3.0mm) 174 (orange)

p.58 **One Point Motifs**

125   • All yarn threads are quadruple.
[1st row] No.25 996 (aqua)/round bead 8/0 (3.0mm), round bead 11/0 (2.2mm) 403 (aqua) & 557 (gold)
[2nd row] No.25 996 (aqua)/round bead 8/0 (3.0mm), round bead 11/0 (2.2mm) 23 (aqua), 557 (gold)
[3rd row] No.25 996 (aqua) /round bead 8/0 (3.0mm) 23 (aqua), 557 (gold), round bead 11/0 (2.2mm) 403 (aqua)
[4th row] No.25 3804 (dark pink) /round bead 8/0 (3.0mm), round bead 11/0 (2.2mm) 553 (pink) & 557 (gold)
[5th row] No.25 3804 (dark pink)/round bead 8/0 (3.0mm), round bead 11/0 (2.2mm) 332 (red purple) & 557 (gold)
[6th row] No.25 3804 (dark pink) /round bead 8/0 (3.0mm) 405 (red), 557 (gold), round bead 11/0 (2.2mm) 332 (red-purple)
[7th row] No.25 917 (pink) /round bead 8/0 (3.0mm), round bead 11/0 (2.2mm) 563 (metallic pink) & 557 (gold)
[8th row] No.25 702 (green) /round bead 8/0 (3.0mm) 7 (green), 557 (gold), round bead 11/0 (2.2mm) 563 (metallic pink)
[9th row] No.25 917 (pink) / round bead 8/0 (3.0mm) 563 (metallic pink), 557 (gold) & round bead 11/0 (2.2mm) 27 (green)

126   • All yarn threads are quadruple.
[1st row] No.25 996 (aqua)/round bead 8/0 (3.0mm) 23 (aqua), 402 (yellow)
[2nd row] No.25 826 (blue)/round bead 8/0 (3.0mm) 403 (aqua) & 557 (gold)
[3rd row] No.25 836 (blue), 917 (pink)/ round bead 8/0 (3.0mm) 23 (aqua), 563 (metallic pink)
[4th row] No.25 3804 (dark pink) /round bead 8/0 (3.0mm) 908 (pink), 332 (red-purple)
[5th row] No.25 3804 (dark pink)/round bead 8/0 (3.0mm) 332 (red-purple), 558 (platinum)
[6th row] No.25 815 (dark red)/round bead 8/0 (3.0mm) 557 (gold), 405 (red)
[7th row] No.25 3607 (pink) /round bead 8/0 (3.0mm) 45 (red), 557 (gold)
[8th row] No.25 917 (pink) /round bead 8/0 (3.0mm) 563 (metallic pink), 557 (gold)
[9th row] No.25 917 (pink) / round bead 8/0 (3.0mm) 27 (green), 557 (gold)

127   • All yarn threads are quadruple.
[1st row] No.25 826 (blue) /round bead 8/0 (3.0mm) 403 (aqua)
[2nd row] No.25 826 (blue) /round bead 8/0 (3.0mm) 23 (aqua)
[3rd row] No.25 3804 (dark pink)/round bead 8/0 (3.0mm) 332 (red-purple)
[4th row] No.25 815 (dark red)/round bead 8/0 (3.0mm) 557 (gold)

[5th row] No.25 3607 (pink) /round bead 8/0 (3.0mm) 563 (metallic pink)
[6th row] No.25 917 (pink) /round bead 8/0 (3.0mm) 27 (green)

128   • All yarn threads are quadruple.
[1st row] No.25 996 (aqua)/6mm-long bugle bead 163 (blue), round bead 11/0 (2.2mm) 557 (gold)
[2nd row] No.25 826 (blue) /6mm-long bugle bead 23 (aqua) / round bead 11/0 (2.2mm) 402 (yellow)
[3rd row] No.25 3804 (dark pink)/6mm-long bugle bead 332 (red purple), round bead 11/0 (2.2mm) 557 (gold)
[4th row] No.25 815 (dark red)/6mm-long bugle bead 332 (red purple) /round bead 11/0 (2.2mm) 402 (yellow)
[5th row] No.25 3607 (pink) /6mm-long bugle bead 45 (red), round bead 11/0 (2.2mm) 557 (gold)
[6th row] No.25 917 (pink) / 6mm-long bugle bead 27 (green), round bead 11/0 (2.2mm) 557 (gold)

129   • All yarn threads are sewing thread #60 (natural undyed color) doubled.
[1st row] hexagonal spangle (5mm, 1/5") 504 (blue), 6mm-long bugle bead 23 (blue), 3mm-long bugle bead 23 (blue), round bead 11/0 (2.2mm) 557 (gold)
[2nd row] hexagonal spangle (5mm, 1/5") 502 (green), 6mm-long bugle bead 27 (green), 3mm-long bugle bead 27 (green), round bead 11/0 (2.2mm) 557 (gold)
[3rd row] hexagonal spangle 5 mm 501 (gold), 6mm-long bugle bead 332 (red-purple), 3mm-long bugle bead 332 (red-purple), round bead 11/0 (2.2mm) 557 (gold), 332 (red-purple)
[4th row] hexagonal spangle 5mm 507 (red), 6mm-long bugle bead 22 (gold), 3mm-long bugle bead 332 (red purple), round bead 11/0 (2.2mm) 557 (gold)
[5th row] hexagonal spangle 5mm 506 (pink), 6mm-long bugle bead 22 (gold), 3mm-long bugle bead 22 (gold), round bead 11/0 (2.2mm) 557 (gold), 563 (metallic pink)
[6th row] hexagonal spangle 5mm 506 (pink), 6mm-long bugle bead 22 (gold), 3mm-long bugle bead 27 (green), round bead 11/0 (2.2mm) 27 (green), 563 (metallic pink)

130   • All yarn threads are sewing thread #60 (natural undyed color) doubled.
[1st row] hexagonal spangle (5mm, 1/5") 504 (blue), 3mm-long bugle bead 22 (gold), round bead 11/0 (2.2mm) 405 (red), 558 (platinum)
[2nd row] hexagonal spangle (5mm, 1/5") 504 (blue), 502 (green), 3mm-long bugle bead 22 (gold), round bead 11/0 (2.2mm) 557 (gold)
[3rd row] hexagonal spangle (5mm, 1/5") 507 (red), 3mm-long bugle bead 22 (gold), round bead 11/0 (2.2mm) 557 (gold)
[4th row] hexagonal spangle (5mm, 1/5") 501 (gold), 3mm-long bugle bead 332 (red purple), round bead 11/0 (2.2mm) 332 (red purple)
[5th row] hexagonal spangle 5mm 506 (pink), round bead 11/0 (2.2mm) 22 (gold), round bead 11/0 (2.2mm) 557 (gold)
[6th row] hexagonal spangle 5mm 506 (pink), 506 (green), 3mm-long bugle bead 27 (green), round bead 11/0 (2.2mm) 557 (gold)

Authors' Profiles

Yasuko Endo

Yasuko started her carrier as a fashion planner for the planning department of an apparel manufacturer, and later turned a freelance designer. She makes craft and home décor designs and products for CRK design, a book and production design firm made up of six graphic designers. She has also appeared on a NHK program, *Sutekini Handmade*, where she presented bead embroidery stitch sample ideas and techniques. Yasuko is based in Japan.

C·R·Kdesign

A unit of six graphic and craft designers, Chiaki Kitaya, Kaoru Emoto, Kuma Imamura, Kumiko Yajima, Yasuko Endo, and Noriko Yoshiue. With their abundant ideas, they are involved in a wide range of activities from planning, production, book design/editing, to photography direction/coordination. Publications include: *Bead Embroidery Stitch Samples, The Beaded Edge: Inspired Designs for Crocheted Edgings and Trims published* by Interweave Press. They are based in Japan.

URL: www.crk-design.com